MERELY
Colossal

THE STORY OF THE MOVIES
FROM THE LONG CHASE
TO THE CHAISE LONGUE

BY

ARTHUR MAYER

DRAWINGS BY GEORGE PRICE

Simon and Schuster
1953

MANUFACTURED IN THE UNITED STATES OF AMERICA
BY AMERICAN BOOK-STRATFORD PRESS, INC., NEW YORK

ACKNOWLEDGMENT

No ONE could write a book about the early days of the movies without constant reference to Terry Ramsaye's *A Million and One Nights,* published and copyright 1926, by Simon and Schuster, Inc. I, like my predecessors, have pilfered freely from Terry—so freely that it would be close to impossible to record it on every occasion—but at least I acknowledge my debt with gratitude and affection.

If Ramsaye is the indispensable historian of the industry, *Variety,* of course, is its Bible. Much of its salty wisdom has been gathered in the best-selling *Show Biz,* copyright 1951, by Abel Green and Joe Laurie, Jr., and published by Henry Holt & Co. I am indebted to its editor, Abel Green, not only for the title of this book but also for permission to borrow freely from both the weekly and the compilation.

Valuable books about our picture pioneers which I have used freely with the permission of the publishers, authors, or authors' agents to refresh my memory are:

Continuous Performance, the Story of A. J. Balaban, as told to his wife, Carrie Balaban, copyright 1942, published by G. P. Putnam's Sons.

Never Let the Weather Interfere, copyright 1946, by Messmore Kendall and published by Farrar, Straus and Young.

Phantom Fame by Harry Reichenbach, as told to David Freedman, copyright 1932 and published by Simon and Schuster, Inc.

The House That Shadows Built, copyright 1928 by Will Irwin and published by Doubleday & Co.

I have also availed myself of other books whose publishers unfortunately are no longer in business and whose consent consequently could not be secured: Edward Dean Sullivan's *The Fabulous Mizner,* published by The Henkle Company; *The Story of the Films* (a series of lectures delivered at Harvard University by film leaders), published by A. W. Shaw Company; and Benjamin Hampton's *History of the Movies,* published by Covici Friede & Company.

I am also appreciative of the courtesy of *Harper's* magazine in permitting me to use material from two of my articles, "Premature Obituary," published July, 1944, and "Myths and Movies," published June, 1951; to *Esquire* for the use of material in my article "Sense and Censorship," published October, 1950; to the *Saturday Review of Literature* for the use of material contained in my article "Are Movies Better Than Ever," originally published June 17, 1950, and to *Theatre Arts* magazine for the use of material in two articles, "People to People," published June, 1946, and "Disquiet on the Western Front," published May, 1950.

I am also grateful to *The New York Times* for permission to adapt material written by me but printed originally over a period of several years in *The New York Times* Drama Section in the form of interviews. In addition to these, I should mention a piece about the history of the Rialto corner entitled "Roll Out the Barrel" by Ted Strauss which appeared in the *Times* Sunday Drama Section, April 20, 1941.

FOREWORD

I have tried to tell the story of the men among whom I have spent my life and who have made the movie industry "Merely Colossal." In the telling, I have tried to show them as they really are—not the crass, vulgar illiterates that wise-cracking dramatists and frustrated authors have depicted, nor the gilded, stuffed statesmen that their publicists and paid biographers have portrayed.

Like most pioneers, they built with whatever means came to hand—and they built according to the mores of their day, which are no longer the mores of today, much as the mores of today will surely not be those of tomorrow.

To love men you must be able to laugh at their foibles; to admire them you must be able to understand their weaknesses. It is with a heart full of such affection and admiration that I have written this book.

A. M.

LIST OF ILLUSTRATIONS

LIST OF ILLUSTRATIONS

x

· I ·

I STRAYED into the motion picture business through a blunder, achieved my first promotion through a blunder and have prospered in moderation ever since then through a series of immoderate blunders. Although I do not entirely string along with the industry wisecrack that "nothing succeeds like failure" it seems to me to come closer to the facts of life than the school of success through thrift and toil on which I was reared—at least to the facts of movie life, as I have found them. For example:

Thomas Edison invented a contraption by which pictures appeared to move. He thought so little of its financial possibilities that he declined to take out foreign patents when he found that the cost might run as high as a hundred and fifty dollars.

Edwin Porter, an ex-sailor, later to produce a one-reel

milestone in pictures, *The Great Train Robbery*, was trying out his hand as a photographer during one of Sir
Thomas Lipton's many bids for the America's Cup.
Crowded out of position by the other cameramen, Porter
had no alternative but to photograph the *Shamrock II*
against the sun, and to his amazement and to the enlight-
enment of all future cameramen, took pictures of striking
backlighted luminosity.

Independent picture producers sought to infringe or
flout the patents on movie cameras, projectors and other
movie-making paraphernalia held by the Motion Picture
Patents Company in New York. The outlaws, constantly
molested in the East, fled to the West Coast, where they
established the motion picture industry not because of the
famous sunlight but because California was three thousand miles away from the patent company's lawyers, and
Los Angeles was close to the Mexican border with easily
accessible refuge from process servers and camera smashers.

Hughey Mack, an early comedian, slipped into the
movies when he malingered on a minor job and fell asleep.
A director heard him snoring, looked at him, admired what
he saw and heard, and woke him up to sign a contract.

Warner Brothers were in severe financial straits. In desperation they experimented with sound co-ordinated with
film, rejected by all the more prosperous producers. As a
consequence, they revitalized the entire industry via Vitaphone, and converted their own cash status from an annual
loss of millions to a profit of seventeen million in 1929.

To persuade Mauritz Stiller, a distinguished Swedish
director, to come to America, Metro-Goldwyn-Mayer per-

The director was so impressed with his snoring he awakened him to sign a contract.

mitted him to bring with him a young actress. Stiller never quite made the grade. The young actress was Greta Garbo.

The pages of motion picture history are studded with hundreds of similar stories of success predicated more on luck than logic. Men have been catapulted into the industry from every walk of life—from pushcart peddler to railroad financier—but few have entered it with less preparation or intent than I, and fewer have survived with less cosmic consequences.

The steps leading to my entry are brief. I went to Harvard College, where, if I acquired any reputation, it was for trying to make more teams and periodicals and lovely ladies and being rejected more promptly by all of them than any living undergraduate. On my last day, however, I did achieve one lean and dubious honor; I was Commencement Day Orator. This was my sole collegiate distinction but strange as it may seem it was my first step toward my motion picture career.

Shortly after graduating I met a young man whose ideals and aims in life were as pure, clear and lofty as my own; we both wanted to make a fortune as rapidly and with as little work as possible. We concocted a scheme which, except for fifteen or twenty major oversights and miscalculations, was basically sound. Every young blade in those days wanted a "genuine" Panama hat; Panama hats, being made under water, could scarcely be subject to mass production; ergo, we could easily corner the market. We pooled our dreams and our dough.

Unfortunately, Panama hats are not made in Panama any more than they are made under water. This belated discovery somewhat undermined the basic structure of our plan, but with the resilience of youth we rode the jolt and forged heroically ahead. Our eventual downfall was due to a more disconcerting and disillusioning revelation—the addiction of the peasantry of foreign lands to hard work. The capacity of the weavers of Ecuador and Peru to produce bordered on fanaticism. For every thousand hats we imported from these frenzied beavers, another two thousand immediately became available. Cornering their output was like trying to catch a school of romantically driven, upstreaming salmon with a shoehorn. Had every young blade in America wanted one of our hats and had every young blade in America had two heads to wear them on, we would still have gone broke.

My commercial self-confidence evaporated along with my bank account and I came to the sad but not unendurable conclusion that I was no businessman. Thirty years in the motion picture business as a theatre operator, publicist, distributor and importer have done nothing to undermine that early conviction.

On leaving the hat-cornering business I met another young man whose ideals and aims in life were as pure, clear and lofty as my own. We both wanted to get away from the sordid world of commerce; we both felt that man's soul required nourishment at our hands. An art gallery of our own seemed the most suitable vocation for dedicated men like ourselves. Pushing the long hair back from our eyes, we looked at the matter realistically. There was, we conceded, no getting away from it: even an art gallery needed the stuff—money.

I called on an eminent banker whom I had known from childhood, and with apparently more vehemence than lucidity confided to him my hopes and plans. He listened to me with undivided inattention. He was himself deeply interested in pictures, he assured me at the end of our brief interview, and gave me a letter of introduction to a man whom he described as America's leading authority on the subject and to whom the du Ponts, with an assist from his bank, were loaning several million dollars.

With such financial support I played with visions of a Renaissance of art in America with myself at its helm. On a hopeful May morning in 1919, in his Fifth Avenue office adorned with portraits of the five glamorous M's of his enterprise—Mabel Normand, Mae Marsh, Madge Kennedy, Mary Garden and Maxine Elliott—Samuel Goldwyn of Goldwyn Pictures read my letter of introduction to him, spoke about three sentences and I was no longer a patron of the arts. The crucial words, if I recall them correctly, were, "If you're such a good talker you ought to make a good salesman." Since I had spoken only three words, "Good morning, sir," I was puzzled, but before I had time to answer further or ask, he pressed a buzzer and called in his assistant, who led me out by the arm. I had been hired as a salesman for neither oils nor etchings but for Goldwyn Motion Pictures. It was not until several days later that I found out what had happened. My banker sponsor, in desperation to find any cogent recommendation for me in the picture industry as he knew it, had dug up my sole collegiate distinction, my Commencement Day oration, and had augmented it in his letter to Goldwyn to read,

"Arthur is a very fine orator. In his four years at Harvard he won the twelve top oratory awards."

In 1919, Goldwyn was not yet the legendary character that his own talents, reinforced by astute publicists, were later to make him. The undertones of Mrs. Malaprop, attributed to him for sound commercial reasons, had not attained their full bloom nurtured by inspired press agents like Lynn Farnol and Jock Lawrence. And it was, of course, many, many years before Ben Sonnenberg was to be called in to undo the legend with equal competence, greater remuneration, and bearing a more impressive title. Sonnenberg is not a press agent. He is a Public Relations Counsel.

Goldwyn did, however, have a native gift for trenchant misstatement. "Include me out" (on resigning from the Will Hays organization) and "a verbal contract isn't worth the paper it's written on" are solid Goldwyn and have deservedly earned their niche in the world of literature, alongside the immortal words of Joe Jacobs, the fight manager; to wit, "I should have stood in bed" and "We wuz robbed," uttered after his property, Max Schmeling, had lost a verdict to Jack Sharkey.

A reliable friend of mine vouches for the authenticity of an earlier work of Goldwyn's, the *Captive* story. This is the one wherein Sam was warned by an associate not to produce *The Captive* because its leading character was a Lesbian. "We'll get around that," Sam airily answered. "We'll make her an American." Such a so-called Goldwynism is credible to me not so much for Sam's unfamiliarity with the vagaries of Eros but as an indication of his grasshopper agility as a story editor.

9

One of my few claims to distinction within the industry is that I am apparently the only person in it who—man or boy—never heard Sam utter a Goldwynism. I was, however, in on the ground floor of one. He advised me once, "First you have a good story, then a good treatment, and next a first-rate director. After that you hire a competent cast and even then you have only the nucleus of a good picture." Since then I have seen this story so often in print rewritten by press agents to "only the mucus of a good picture" that I now tell it that way myself. Actually, Sam not only said "nucleus," but he pronounced all three syllables with the precision and pear-shaped tones of a Redpath Chautauqua elocutionist. I make this statement not in defense of Sam but to redeem my amateur standing.

That a first-rate publicity representative can often improve on the original product, however, cannot be denied, and there is no higher example than the curtain line of the celebrated meeting between Goldwyn and George Bernard Shaw during which Sam tried to sell Shaw on the idea of coming to Hollywood. "The trouble, Mr. Goldwyn, is that you are only interested in art," Shaw is supposed to have said, "and I am only interested in money." As an ardent admirer of the great vegetarian I am, nevertheless, pleased to report that the real author of that neat and excellent line was the rare-steak eater, publicist and lyrist, Howard Dietz, who was at the time working for Goldwyn.

Goldwyn's attitude toward publicity on the whole was simple, logical and, granted his postulates, unimpeachable: people wanted art in pictures. The Goldwyn touch was art. For their own good, people should hear about the Goldwyn who brought the Goldwyn touch to pictures. Press agents should keep people's minds from wandering off the subject of Goldwyn the artist. There is a story, quite untrue, like most Goldwyn fables, but not entirely untypical of the great man, that one of his henchmen once wrote an ad for a forthcoming picture which read simply, "The directorial skill of Mamoulian, the radiance of Anna Sten and the genius of Goldwyn have united to make the world's greatest entertainment."

"That," Sam is supposed to have said, "is the kind of ad I like. Facts. No exaggeration."

From the outset of his career, Goldwyn was convinced that the writer was the foundation on which good pictures must be established, and in his early years he touchingly believed that the bigger the name the better the writer. Accordingly he corralled such eminent authors of the day as Maurice Maeterlinck, Robert W. Chambers, Rex Beach, Rupert Hughes, Gertrude Atherton, Gouverneur Morris and others whose talents were even less cinematic. If neither Goldwyn nor the screen was permanently enriched by their writings, no one could deny that Goldwyn had not classed up the industry.

In his early days he was also impressed with distinguished stage names but unfortunately the industry's Number One cornerer, Adolph Zukor, having entered the field before him, had already signed up the most luminous. Among the few who had resisted Zukor and who were cajoled into pictures at great expense by Goldwyn were Mary Garden, Jane Cowl and Maxine Elliott. Regrettably their talents were ill suited to the screen and their maturity led Goldwyn kibitzers to refer to his stable as "The Old Ladies' Home." Their photographs in publications, however (looking admiringly at Sam), attracted a public which had previously looked down on the movies and had never, to his amazement, even heard of Goldwyn, so that his ladies were not, as investments go, a total loss.

A press agent friend of mine who worked for Goldwyn in his earlier days told me that Goldwyn himself picked the adjectives to use in conjunction with publicizing his stars. Maxine Elliott was "dignified." Mary Garden was "elegant," Jane Cowl "soulful," Madge Kennedy was "winsome," Geraldine Farrar "glamorous," Mae Marsh was "the whim girl," and Mabel Normand "vivacious." The soulful Miss Cowl and the dignified Miss Elliott lasted scarcely long enough for my friend to translate Goldywn adjectives into Goldwyn advertising. The winsome Madge Kennedy was easy; she read *Science and Health with Key to the Scriptures* between shootings on the set, and was the kind of a girl who once refused to enter a scene through a dumbwaiter because the step down would expose her legs above the ankle. She also once rejected a Turkish costume until it was stitched and draped to conceal any indelicate indication of the presence of pants underneath. (Today we discreetly urge Hollywood to indicate their absence.)

Applying the correct adjectives to other favorites in the Goldwyn harem of his day, however, must occasionally have taxed his inventiveness. I once heard the elegant Garden say—about a supposedly very virile director who was part Indian—"I love Carewe. He spits on the floor." And when Enrico Caruso made his unsuccessful debut in *My*

Cousin, I recall hearing the glamorous Farrar gloatingly announce, "The spaghetti-eater's picture was a flop at the Rivoli."

On another occasion I remember that the publicity department arranged for the vivacious Mabel Normand to be interviewed by a sedate family magazine writer. When asked by the interviewer what she liked most, Mabel answered, "I love dark, windy days when trees break and houses creak." The interviewer noted these passionate words on a pad. When asked next what her hobbies were, she said, "I don't know. Say anything you like but don't say I like to work. That sounds like Mary Pickford, that prissy bitch. Just say I like to pinch babies and twist their legs. And get drunk."

Goldwyn was inducted into the motion picture business in the early 1900's through love. As a glove salesman he fell for the charms of a cornet player, Miss Blanche Lasky, who, with her brother, Jesse L. Lasky, also a cornet player, was the lead in a vaudeville act called "The Musical Laskys." He persuaded Miss Lasky to become Mrs. Samuel Goldwyn, or Goldfish, which was then his name.

As a result of this merger the Lasky Company was formed. The partners rented a barn in Hollywood and their first picture was *The Squaw Man* with Dustin Farnum starring and Cecil B. DeMille directing. It proved so profitable that it started Lasky, DeMille and Goldwyn on their fabulously successful careers.

In 1917 Adolph Zukor, president of the Famous Players Company, merged his company with the Lasky Company, forming Famous Players-Lasky. Lasky took over the pro-

duction end of the business but between Goldwyn and
Zukor it was announced that there were "business and
personal differences." Knowing the two gentlemen I can
easily believe there were. It has also been reported that
Goldwyn was given a million dollars in cash by Zukor for
his exit. Knowing Zukor, I personally doubt it. In 1918
Goldwyn formed Goldwyn Pictures with Archie and Edgar
Selwyn. When I met him he had just emerged from this
unsuccessful venture. Archie Selwyn complained that his
erstwhile associate, Goldfish, had not only lost most of
Selwyn's money but had appropriated half of his name.

Over the years Goldwyn has had the highest batting
average of any living producer. He has been responsible
for occasional potboilers but he has to his credit such
memorable films as *Dodsworth, Wuthering Heights, Stella
Dallas, The Little Foxes, Dead End,* and one of the four
top grossing pictures of all times, *The Best Years of Our
Lives,* exceeded only in receipts by *Birth of a Nation, Gone
With the Wind,* and *Samson and Delilah.* He was, moreover (and still is), one of the few picture producers who was
an expert not only in making pictures but in their distribution, publicizing and sale to the public. In this, like the
description of Alexander Woollcott, Goldwyn was "a sensitive, creative artist with a fine sense of double-entry book-
keeping."

Although employed as a salesman within five minutes
after entering Goldwyn's office, it was several weeks before
I actually hit the road. This was due to the fact that after
the first day nobody could remember what I had been
hired for. This was a natural state of affairs in the picture

business of those days, and I might have stayed in the home office for years had I not taken matters into my own hands. Hanging around, picking up scraps of information, lore and gossip, watching the screening of new films in the projection rooms, observing charmers like Mabel Normand flit in and out, I became ambitious. I decided I was much too gifted for a salesman's job; that I rightly belonged in the production end of the business; that I was, after all, fundamentally a creative spirit like Goldwyn himself and that I should be in Hollywood.

I was attacked by visions of "Arthur Mayer Pictures" in gold on an office door, and I started to dream of such future newspaper plaudits as "Arthur Mayer has done it again" and "Without question, Arthur Mayer is the century's leading producer of quality pictures" and "Let's face it, when we want Art there is only one Art Mayer." Spurred by these and other even less modest aspirations, perhaps inspired by a nod from Miss Normand, I boldly entered Goldwyn's office one morning to take the matter up with him. With my belt tightened and my hair slicked back, I presented my case with such eloquence that he was immediately reminded of my reputed oratorical powers and that I had been taken on as a salesman. He again pressed a buzzer, called in his assistant and demanded to know why the hell I was still loafing around wasting my talents and his money. The assistant, who had not seen me since the first day he led me out, said he would "look it up." While he was doing this I made a last, wistful pitch to Goldwyn for Hollywood. His final, adamant answer was, "Hollywood is the place to go only after you've learned the business." That was thirty-three years ago. Except for a number of brief visits, Hollywood has had to struggle along without the benefit of my genius. And I am still learning the business.

· II ·

EXHIBITIONS OF "living pictures" started before the turn of the century and were housed in penny arcades. I have a vivid recollection of the early arcades on Fourteenth Street in New York City where I was taken as a boy by Grandpa. I liked the leather-lunged barkers out front whose antics I was to copy forty years later at my own Rialto Theatre uptown at Broadway and Forty-second Street, and I liked the garish front displays I was also in time to outgarish. I liked the smell, the bustle, the eager patrons waiting their turn to look through the peephole at the pictures; I liked everything about the arcades, in fact, but the living pictures. A typical program was a series of shorts made up of such excessively dull subject matter as a scene from the coronation of the Czar of Russia, surf crashing on the shores of Dover, a bathing pier at Nice and strolling ladies with their skirts being blown high enough daringly to show their ankles.

My idea of hot entertainment was the kind put out by the Eden Musée on Twenty-third Street. When the movies became an added attraction there, I ignored them, continuing to throw my business to the old acts like the Gallery of Mirrors which showed passers-by as very fat or very thin and the Chamber of Horrors in the basement where there were waxworks displays of such enthralling spectacles as a man about to be electrocuted, captured revolutionists being trampled on by elephants and the Chicago anarchists planning the destruction of society.

If anyone had predicted to me that these wonders would be relegated to the Coney Islands of the world while the flickers would go on to flourish and be lavishly housed in palaces, I would have considered it only another instance of adult stupidity.

Terry Ramsaye, the indispensable historian of the industry, reports on another critic of the early films, a respectable financial backer of one of the arcades. At his request records of the daily receipts were produced for him one day which showed the following break-down:

> U. S. Battleship at Sea—25¢
> Joseph Jefferson in Rip's Sleep—43¢
> Ballet Dancer—$1.05
> Girl Climbing Apple Tree—$3.65

"I think," said the financier, soundly forecasting the future of movie production, "we'd better have some more of the girl-climbing-apple-tree kind."

Hour of decision. Here was my life's calling.

19

I never saw Girl Climbing Apple Tree but there was undoubtedly more of her exposed than in my ladies' skirts being blown high enough to show their ankles. I say this in self-vindication because I don't like to think that the financier outvisioned me on the screen or in the future. Had I seen her I might have preferred her to the Chamber of Horrors and backed sex instead of crime in my future film career. On the other hand I was not altogether a flop as a seer. Over the years crime and comedy have been romance's closest contenders at the box office; they have, in fact, and at certain periods, run such a close race that a photo finish was needed to determine the winner. With due respect to sex as a revenue producer, I can at least truthfully report that crime also pays.

Living pictures were first shown in a regular or legitimate theatre in 1896 at Koster and Bial's Music Hall, a well-known New York vaudeville theatre standing where Macy's is now located, then the center of Broadway night life. The great moguls of vaudeville, however, with the complacency of success, persisted in regarding living pictures as a temporary fad whose novelty would soon be exhausted. They were used in the vaudeville houses as "chasers" between shows to drive out the patrons. Indeed, the history of motion pictures might well be summarized to date as starting with drive-outs and culminating with drive-ins.

While vaudeville and big business saw nothing in pictures, the arcade owners did; they scented a heaven-sent opportunity to acquire riches through selling cheap entertainment to the masses, and the first rudimentary motion picture theatres started when these little visionaries began to partition off the rears of their stores and equip them with screens and chairs to seat anywhere from fifty to one hundred patrons.

The arcade owners came almost exclusively from humble walks of life. They were traveling salesmen, racetrack touts, and small fur merchants like Adolph Zukor and Marcus Loew; another future movie magnate, William Fox, was a cloth sponger. A little later in the field were other future tycoons such as the Warner brothers, who converted a store in Newcastle, Pennsylvania, into a theatre for which they borrowed chairs from an undertaking establishment. When there was a funeral their patrons had to stand. Still another was Carl Laemmle, a small-town Wisconsin clothing store manager whose dream was to move to the big city of Chicago. On a reconnoitering trip there in search of a new haberdashery connection he found instead a picture show house which had been abandoned in such haste by its former owners in flight from their creditors that they had left behind them the screen, the kitchen chairs and even a roll of unused tickets. All a new owner needed to be in business was a projection machine, some film and some customers. Laemmle got them.

Thomas Tally of Los Angeles, a former cowboy, was another of the pioneers. He forsook his ponies for a picture store and overcame the skepticism of potential customers by cutting a peephole through which transients could get a free glimpse inside of the life-size images in motion. With this strip-tease technique he lured the dubious to pay to sit inside where they could enjoy a complete view of the latest miracle. When his customers first saw a picture of a railroad train rushing directly toward them they screamed with horror and men and women in the first rows dashed for the door to escape destruction. After a dancing short, mashers would hang around the exit hoping to date up the girls. Tally was later, in 1900, to open the Electric Theatre, the first exclusive emporium for the showing of films in Los Angeles. Fifty years later the entire industry commemorated this opening in the *Movietime, U.S.A.* publicity campaign which I helped organize and conduct.

In 1905 John P. Harris—whose son is now a popular figure in industry activities—remodeled a storeroom in McKeesport, Pennsylvania, and opened it as a moving picture theatre, christening it a nickelodeon ("odeon" from the Greek for theatre and nickel from the belief that five cents, a four-cent hoist from a penny, was all the traffic would bear).

For his première Harris showed *The Great Train Robbery,* which for plot can still hold its own in the wholesale murder school, concerning which I claim to be the world's foremost authority.

It opens with a bunch of bandits on horseback riding hell-bent for a lonely depot. Inside the depot they knock the agent cold, hog-tie him and over his telegraph key (one of the bandits handily happens to know the Morse code) they send out a signal which halts an on-rushing train at the siding outside. They hold up the train crew, blow up the safe, kill the messenger and are about to kill all the passengers when the agent's little daughter, bringing the supper pail to Papa, discovers his condition, frees and re-

vives him and notifies the sheriff, who with his men quickly
provide the "chase." Finally the sheriff's men close in on
the bandits, who fight to the death behind their fallen
horses. When the last man has rolled over dead and there
isn't an upright character left, the story seems, of necessity,
to be finished. But not at all. A masked and menacing
bandit suddenly comes to, leaps to his feet, draws his gun
and shoots five bullets straight at the audience. The End.

The first day Harris took in $22.50, the next day $76.00.
News of this gold mine spread immediately and from one
end of America to the other, hundreds of entrepreneurs
began to convert storerooms, barns and any space available
into theatres. Theatres multiplied like rabbits. Within
three years there were four thousand. Movie-going rapidly
became part of the mores of the majority of city and town
folks and the development of the automobile and the
building of hard roads made fans out of farmers. Passionate
professional lovers on the screen brought new and improved standards of kissing and petting to the farmer's
daughter, who was, by this time, I assume, pretty fed up
with the technique of traveling salesmen.

With affluence and competition, refinements began to
appear. "Stamped metal fronts" was one. For $1500 you
could buy a very gaudy front that ran well above the first
floor. Stamped metal was for permanent or semipermanent
theatres; transients or get-it-while-you-can operators used
lithograph fronts. This innovation has been credited to
old "Pop" Lubin of Philadelphia, one of the most successful of the early producers. After a long and active career,
however, Pop was still not convinced that he was in the

right business. "I was a fool to go into making movies instead of producing plays," he told a friend. "In the theatre an actor can rush on stage and yell, 'The ship has sunk with all on board!' In the movies you have to spend five thousand dollars to show the ship sinking. And actors can get drowned yet and sue you."

Interiors were likewise considered and efforts made to pretty them up. When the air became too oppressive it would be deodorized by a hand sprayer such as is used in a garden. You could get this spray by the gallon for fifty cents and in a variety of odors but whether it was heliotrope, verbena or geranium there was still no illusion of sitting in a garden. Benches and undertakers' chairs were replaced by tip-up chairs with veneer seats and backs and in the cities pipe organs replaced the piano. Credit for this musical milestone has been claimed by many. The ex-cowboy, Thomas Tally, is among those who insist they were the first; and Adolph Zukor is reported to have installed one as early as 1910 in connection with *The Passion Play* in Newark, New Jersey, where he brought the wrath of the church down on his head for using the sacred instrument in a nickelodeon. There is no doubt as to who eventually introduced the flashy three-console organ; it was, of course, and it could have been no other: "Roxy."

When Goldwyn sent me out to try my persuasive powers on theatre owners, known as exhibitors, it was not to the cities but to rural and small-town communities in the Middle West where improvements and refinements had progressed little further than Harris' McKeesport nickelodeon. Most of the theatres were family affairs. The Missus sold tickets, one daughter collected them at the door with one hand and vended home-made taffy with the other. Another daughter played suitable accompaniments on a usually out-of-tune piano. One son showed patrons to their seats and tried to control unruly children who darted up and down the poorly lit aisles; another son ran the projection machine, often inserting a reel upside down, and looked after the constantly recurring mechanical breakdowns. The "One minute please" slide was considered standard equipment, bought along with the projector.

All Papa had to do was buy the film, drive around the countryside putting up posters, arrange for window cards in store windows in exchange for passes, and at night after the "Good night" slide was put away, count up the day's take. After that he went home with his unpaid female and child labor employees, who cooked his supper for him and made up another batch of candy to sell.

The family was such an integral part of early theatre operations that one sonless exhibitor on whom I called offered me a half interest in his theatre if I would marry his daughter. I took one look at the lady and departed hurriedly, leaving him sole proprietor of both.

Illustrated slides were still a feature in those communities and primitive humor was appreciated; You Wouldn't Spit on the Floor at Home, Don't Do It Here, or Ladies, We Like Your Hats but Please Remove Them, or a set of local ads like You Feed Yourself but Let Us Feed Your Livestock, They're More Valuable . . . Harry's Grain and Oats Co.

Popular mood music numbers were "At Dawning,"

"Somewhere a Voice Is Calling," "The Sunshine of Your Smile," "Pony Boy," "Just A-Wearyin' for You," "Poor Butterfly," "The William Tell Overture," and the sign-off number was invariably "When You Come to the End of a Perfect Day." I heard those numbers so often that when I hear them today I automatically start shilling for Goldwyn.

Film subtitles had progressed from NEXT MORNING and CAME THE DAWN to purple lyrics like PASSION, THAT FURIOUS TASKMASTER, STRIKES WITHOUT WARNING AND LEAVES THE MARK OF ITS LASH ACROSS THE SOUL. But most disarming of all was the subtitle of an early Ramon Novarro movie. As the romantic Latin clasped his sweetheart to his breast and sailed his canoe down the raging rapids, the caption read DOWN THE VIRGIN FALLS.

As a salesman I worked out of one of the Goldwyn exchanges or what would be called in any other industry a branch office. The word "exchanges" was brought into the vocabulary of the industry at an early date. When the first films were produced they were bought outright; after showing them the theatre owners would "exchange" them with one another in simple neighborly fashion. Simplicity and neighborly love are virtues which have rarely flourished for long in my business; in fact, this is the only instance I recall of their ever even existing, and it was indeed of short duration.

The owners quickly pulled themselves together and started charging one another a small rental. In this fashion they made a little extra money which flagrantly violated a producer tradition even then firmly established—that the best customer is a hungry one. Producers promptly discontinued selling film and themselves began to rent. They subsequently established their own exchanges in each of the major cities of the country. Out of these, salesmen traveled and called on exhibitors; films were shipped to the exhibitors, examined on their return for defects and then reshipped to other exhibitors. Also, exchanges sold advertising accessories ranging from 8 x 10 stills to 24-sheets.

The exchange setup, enlarged to approximately thirty-two for each company, is about the same in function today as it was then, but with the passage of the years, their operations have been established on a reasonably efficient basis. In my early days, however, they were conducted with a complete lack of competent supervision and a considerable amount of efficient knavery.

Being a greenhorn from the East and suspected by the exchange managers of being an office pet or, even worse, a relative of somebody high up, I was given the works. I was sent on long train rides to far-flung hamlets where theatres were known to be closed, overbooked or operating only two days a week, and my calling list was confined almost exclusively to exhibitors avowedly hostile to Goldwyn. Even in those days there were many who suspected Sam of an unforgivable weakness for art, not to mention high film rentals.

It should be made clear that exhibitors, chastened by experience if not by natural instinct, have always been allergic to anything aesthetic and their most damning description of a film is that it is "artistic." The mere mention of the word in their presence can often make them break out with occupational hives and invectives. Their resentment not only applies to film but also to advertising accessories. I remember one theatre owner who complained that a poster he had just received from the exchange was too highbrow. I looked at it hanging in his lobby. It was a picture of a girl in a jungle. Behind a tree was a tiger with full denture exposed, drooling, and crouched for the pounce. Behind another tree was the lustful, drooling villain with a club in his hand and, himself, also ready to pounce. The girl was holding a dagger to her bare breast preparatory to taking her own life if the worse came to the worst, which seemed both highly likely and highly imminent. The idea was that if the tiger didn't get her, the dagger would, and her chastity would be happily preserved. I asked the exhibitor what he objected to. "It's too pretty," he complained. "It's got no kick to it. I like posters with some action." I asked him what he called action. "A lot of dead bodies laying around dead" was his definition.

In another lobby, listening to another exhibitor's complaints about the pastel content of a poster, I lightly suggested that we could gory it up by throwing a bucket of blood across it. His eyes brightened with enthusiasm and admiration. "That's it," he exclaimed, "that's just what it needs. That'll bring 'em in." His enthusiasm for gore, which must have been infectious, and his high endorsement of me as an art editor must have registered, because years later I used exactly the same technique at my own Rialto. I confined myself to red paint, however; paint is cheaper, holds its color longer and smells better. Anyhow, it brought 'em in.

Many of the most articulate salesmen as well as their customers were ex-carnival spielers or graduate medicine men with an amazing capacity to manipulate film as artfully as walnut shells. Almost invariably they were warmhearted and simple-minded men with a rare insight into human conduct and emotions, seamy or exemplary. As a consequence of their companionship and admonitions, I acquired a permanent advantage over many motion picture executives who, although far more experienced and talented than I, had never lived closely with the men who sell pictures to the exhibitors, or the exhibitors who sell them to the public.

I remember with particular affection a fountain of profane wisdom popularly known as Sockless Sam. He had acquired that sobriquet because summer and winter he wore spats, and the simple deduction was that he wore them instead of socks. Sam had run away from home at an early age—earlier each time he mentioned it—to join a traveling circus. What he did in the days of his novitiate varied also in the telling and with the amount of liquor he had been consuming. Apparently, however, after distinguishing himself in a series of hey-Rube battles with unappreciative rural communities, he became a carnival spieler for a half-lady and half-man attraction and later an itinerant salesman for a Spanish fly preparation in whose aphrodisiac virtues he retained a touching faith plus a few cases of the product. Like many more distinguished publicists he eventually came to believe in his own concoctions. He even made me believe in them one night, when I was in an experimental mood. The result was that my stomach thought I had swallowed a lighted firecracker. In the interests of scientific research I feel obligated to report that the sensation confined itself to that latitude.

With a show-business background of this piebald nature, Sam had early scented the money-making possibilities of the movies. Inspired by a show that he chanced to see with some jerky views of his hero, Teddy Roosevelt, Carrie Nation smashing a saloon and a favorite short of the day, considered highly risqué, called *How Bridget Served the Salad Undressed,* he had promptly borrowed or stolen enough capital to rent a small store show. The pictures were projected on a white muslin sheet. Projectors were cranked by hand with the film feeding through the apparatus into a basket underneath (the automatic film rewind was yet to be invented) and the seats were wooden benches. But these crudities had been offset by a king-size player piano with a lighted art glass front with built-in cymbals that played the same giant roll over and over again, furnishing a by no means invariably appropriate musical accompaniment.

Business was good and Sam was making money when catastrophe overtook him. One day there was a fire in the booth and all of his equipment, seats, screen and his beloved piano went up in flame. He had no insurance because in his day only the most foolhardy of insurance brokers would risk anything as inflammable as celluloid. Or Sam. When I met him he had got himself a selling job with one of the then small distributors, Warner Brothers. The Warners have always been enterprising. They were so enterprising that they emigrated from Russia when

Harry, the oldest, was only six years old, and their rise to fame and fortune is in the best American tradition. With all of their ingenuity, however, and with all of their familiarity with enterprise in its many forms, I think that even they might have been surprised had they heard their inventive employee in his pitches urging exhibitors to "Beware of foreigners like Zukor or Fox, friend. Patronize a fine old American firm like Warner." Another of his merchandising methods was less imaginative but more profitable. When all else had failed him, Sam would state with feigned candor that there was comparatively little difference between the reels of one company and another; that his were neither better nor worse than the next film peddler's; that they were all, in fact, pretty bad and he was willing to settle the price man to man with any sporting-blooded exhibitor. There were many takers. And it should be added that while his pictures might not have been overladen with talent, Sam and his dice were loaded with it.

Sam took a great fancy to me and his expression of it was daily and fatherly advice. One excellent piece of counsel he gave me early in my selling career was, "It starts early, Artie. For every kid with an honest two bits in his pocket there's six across the street scheming how to get it off him." Another was, "Always tell the truth—no one will believe you. For instance, if another salesman asks you where you're going this week so he can beat you there and you're going to Sheboygan, say so. That's the one place he won't expect to find you." Still another was, "Never trust people with nicknames like 'Honest' Joe or 'Old Reliable.' "

I cherish Sam's memory far above that of many more virtuous and successful citizens.

In those days, films were rented entirely on a basis of negotiation. Hostilities started with a high price asked and a low rental offered. After a prolonged exchange of appropriate insults, a compromise was eventually effected with little regard for the equities of the situation but predicated on the exhibitor's need for a picture versus the salesman's necessity for revenue, a procedure which I might add has in no way since been basically altered.

Another practice was to sell film "sight unseen." This was not only a convenient dodge but a necessity as in most cases the pictures were actually only a glint in some producer's eye or at best in the early stages of production. By court decree today pictures must be publicly screened before they can be offered to exhibitors. Few buyers, however, take advantage of this legal concern over their welfare, preferring to rely on trade paper reviews, trade association reports or just their own instinct. In the absence of such aids, and without even the product, I had to depend on my imagination stimulated only by gaudy booklets more flamboyant than accurate in their descriptions—or prophecies —of stories, titles, stars and supporting casts.

Before leaving New York I had somewhere picked up an impressive phrase, "Rembrandt lighting." I hadn't the faintest idea what it meant but I boasted to buyers that all of my pictures had it. The point was usually received with such apathy that I was never, fortunately, asked to explain it. It was not until years later that I found out what it was from the man who invented it, Cecil B. DeMille. In his early experimental days in Hollywood he had wanted the effect of sun shining on only one side of an actor's face. To get the effect, he had the actor work in the dark and he put an old theatre spotlight on one side of him. For De-Mille the results were gratifying, and highly pleased with himself he rushed the pictures to his company's sales department in New York. After seeing it they promptly wired back, "Have you gone mad? Do you expect us to be able to sell a picture for full price when you only show half a man?" DeMille was desperate, he said, until he was divinely inspired; he telegraphed New York, "If you fellows are so dumb you don't know Rembrandt lighting when you see it, don't blame me." The sales department wired back in exultation, "What a sales argument," and immediately re-christened the picture a "de luxe special" and tripled the price for it.

"Bicycling" by exhibitors was a common practice. Bicycling means that a print of a film would be rented for one theatre by an enterprising theatre owner who controlled or who had friends interested in a few other houses. A print in those days consisted of approximately six reels, each running close to ten minutes. Theatre No. 1 would play the first few reels and then rush them, by bicycle, to theatre No. 2, which would forward them to theatre No. 3 until the entire picture had been shown in all of the theatres. Sometimes, abetted by a friendly salesman or booker, the exhibitor would neglect even to return the print. One theatre manager I knew a good many years later purloined *Scarface*, which he showed to his customers whenever he felt it desirable to avoid paying the rental for a new picture. He did this on at least half a dozen occasions before a patron complained to him, "These gangster pictures seem to be getting more and more alike."

Another expedient of devious salesmen and exhibitors was "duping." This consisted of sending a print to a laboratory and having a negative photographed from the positive. The duped negative could be used to run off additional copies. These were, of course, inferior in quality but good enough to be sold to exigent if not exacting subsequent-run theatres. "Miss-outs" were another common occurrence. As a consequence of the careless manner in which exchanges were operated an exhibitor might get no picture at all, he might get two (one meant for his competitor which he would carefully overlook until it was too late to forward it), or he might receive *Motherhood* when he had booked *The Wages of Sin.*

Duping, incidentally, was such a common practice in the very early days that a man in Brooklyn went into the business and openly sold shares in it. He had netted himself forty thousand dollars before he was apprehended by the first of the committees which the industry periodically organizes to police itself. This group called itself simply "The Film Theft Committee."

"Block booking," the practice of selling pictures in groups rather than individually, was as yet in its infancy, but even then a salesman's objective was to tie in half a dozen obvious palookas with a smash attraction or a picture with a popular performer in it. My major bait one season, I remember, was *The Old Nest*, a mother-love sob story with Richard Dix in the leading role. This I was given explicit instructions never to sell without "wrapping around the exhibitor's neck" three or four Will Rogers features. At that time, Rogers, already recognized by the legitimate stage for his rare value both as a performer and a shrewd commentator on the American scene, was as welcome to the average small-town exhibitor as a smallpox sign in the lobby. One lady operator in the north woods of Wisconsin turned him down with the criticism, "He's too much like home folks. He don't seem like an actor."

When I once asked Rogers in later years what persuaded him to forgo his immensely successful stage career for the uncertainties of the movies, he drawled, "Pictures are the only business where you can sit out front and applaud yourself." In this he was incorrect. A friend of mine once said to Harpo Marx after a stage performance in New York, "Where were you at the third curtain call?" "I was the fellow in the first row," answered the comedian, "clapping so loud."

Another at that time unappreciated performer on our Goldwyn program was Lon Chaney, Sr. Chaney, who was probably the best character actor developed in the movies, attributed his success to his good fortune in having deaf-mutes for his parents. The necessity of communicating with them in childhood laid the basis for his facility in panto-mime. He later became a star overnight in *The Miracle Man*, but when I was peddling him he was in something called *The Penalty*, which, parlayed with Will Rogers' *Jes' Call Me Jim* and *Honest Hutch*, made for feeble competition up against Fox's *Over the Hill*, modestly advertised as "the greatest human drama in the history of the world." It was packaged with such morsels as *The Tiger's Club* with Pearl White and *A Ridin' Romeo* with Tom Mix, and helped, along with some personal deficiencies, to make my debut as a salesman less than sensational. Other disastrous competition was Pola Negri in *Passion*, Mary Miles Minter in *Sweet Lavender*, Sessue Hayakawa in *First Born*, not to mention Mary Pickford, Douglas Fairbanks, Sr., and Charlie Chaplin.

Occasionally I reported back to the New York office and on the occasions of our meeting Goldwyn always addressed me as "My Pupil" (as he still does) and he was encouraging and generous with his praise. No matter what I had done wrong he would invariably put his arm around my shoulder and say, "You're getting along fine." He was, however, equally sanguine with Maurice Maeterlinck. When the distinguished Belgian author left his office after his unsuccessful fling in the movies, Goldwyn put his arm around *his* shoulder. "Don't worry, Maurice," he said, "I'm sure you'll make good yet."

I developed and have over the years retained a huge admiration for Goldwyn's talents and taste. My admiration, unfortunately, was not shared by the bankers and big businessmen who constituted his Board of Directors. He had a predilection for investing their money in a lordly manner unappreciated by them, and his dalliance with art was as culpable in their minds as it was in those of the exhibitors. In 1919 he had the temerity to import from Germany the first futuristic modern art picture ever produced, *The Cabinet of Dr. Caligari*. Its producer was Erich Pommer, the head of UFA, the German film trust. Having produced several expensive pictures, Pommer was seeking to allay criticism by bringing down the average cost of his year's product with a few B pictures. Consequently when a young man named Robert Wiene showed him sketches of some highly modernistic backdrops, Pommer was much impressed (or so he later told me) not so much by their beauty or originality as by their close to negligible cost. No one was more amazed than Pommer that the cheapie he nurtured proved a masterpiece, not to mention a big box-office attraction in Germany.

Today, *Caligari* is cherished all over the world as one of the great landmarks in movie annals as well as the grand-daddy of all horror films. Youthful audiences of aesthetes at New York's Museum of Modern Art screenings still watch it goggle-eyed with breathless appreciation. Back in those days, however, it was regarded by American critics, exhibitors and Goldwyn bankers as "an insult to human intelligence." A couple of trustful theatre owners whom I persuaded to rent it "sight unseen" sued Goldwyn for malicious and wanton damage to their reputations.

As a result of *Caligari* and half a dozen other ways which Goldwyn devised to run amuck with the du Pont millions —and it has been said about him that he is the only man in the world who can run amuck sitting down—a du Pont man was moved onto the premises to try to bring order into the chaos known as Goldwyn Pictures. He was one of the first of the "efficiency experts" hopefully to be imported into the industry by big businessmen under the spell of graphs, charts and diagrams. Such experts have seldom survived for any length of time and on departure almost invariably leave behind them increased losses and more faith than ever by picture people in the hunch rather than the statistical system of operation. As one old-timer once said to me, "I don't want to study no pictures about the picture business."

During the depression of the early thirties, one of the New York banks involved in motion picture financing sent a couple of its experts to Hollywood. They were horrified when they discovered that for every actor who appeared on the screen there were thirteen people at work behind the camera. "This is typical Hollywood extravagance," they wired home. "It must be stopped at once." Six months later the deflated efficiency lads returned to New York. By that time the number of people behind the camera had jumped to seventeen.

During his brief day of authority on the Goldwyn premises, the distressed du Pont delegate looked about him for someone to share his perplexities. The limitations under which he labored are illustrated by the fact that he selected me as his assistant. Although there was nothing in my abbreviated career to justify such a reproach, he referred to me as "the nearest thing to a businessman in the whole crazy outfit."

· III ·

WHILE PERFORMING my new and singular duties I formed
an attachment for a personable young woman with dramatic ambitions. Nightly she tripped daintily into a Broadway drawing room to acquit herself of her five-word part,
"Your bath is drawn, Madam." Fortunately for me,
Madam was washed up in the first act, permitting my
friend to be available for more congenial activities after
nine-fifteen. To kill time, I made a habit of puttering
around the Goldwyn offices until that hour. Occasionally,
I noticed a tall, saturnine figure gliding noiselessly and ob-
servantly about the premises. One night he summoned me
into what had been until that moment Mr. Goldwyn's oak-
paneled office and from whose doors workmen were rapidly
removing the gilded remains of his name. Name removers
were experts at their jobs in those days, for the longevity of

movie executives was limited; some of the more timid were reluctant to leave their offices for a full hour's lunch and the weak-kidneyed were in constant jeopardy.

The stranger, Mr. F. J. (Joe) Godsol, stuck a cigar as thick as three thumbs into my gaping mouth and informed me that Goldwyn and Goldwyn Pictures were no longer synonymous. He advised me further that he was favorably impressed by the ambition and industry of a young man like myself whom he had observed spending long hours of unrewarded overtime at the office. With no further estimate of my suitability for the title and with no increase in salary, I was forthwith appointed his "confidential secretary."

Godsol was a money-making dynamo who, during the First World War, sold spavined mules instead of healthy horses to the French government. He used to quote approvingly ex-Vice-President Dawes' defiant statement, "I'd have paid horse prices for sheep, if the sheep could have hauled artillery." The trouble was, from all accounts, Godsol's mules could hardly haul themselves. As a consequence of this and other business enterprises he was both a multimillionaire and no longer *persona grata* on the European continent.

His major American activity was the sale of Tecla pearls, which he assured me were "much superior to the original." By investing his pearl and mule money in Goldwyn Pictures, he had become, first a member of the Board of Directors, then Chairman of the Board, and when he finally became Goldwyn himself he saw no reason why, following the same recipe for success, he could not produce

"*Goldwyn and Goldwyn Pictures are no longer synonymous!*"
he announced, as he stuck a cigar as big as three thumbs into my
gaping mouth.

much cheaper films than Goldwyn had, and get horse prices for them.

If energy, shrewdness, tenacity and a big bank account spell success, Godsol was Dale Carnegie. He reached the office at seven in the morning and never stopped until one the following day, and he expected the members of his cabinet to keep the same hours. This cabinet consisted of some unusually talented and lovable young men, among them William Rodgers, later vice-president and sales manager of Loew's, Inc.; James Grainger, the future distribution head of Republic Pictures, and the aforementioned G. B. Shaw ghost writer, Howard Dietz.

It was Godsol's habit to hold daily meetings at the ungodly hour of eight o'clock in the morning; it was also his habit to pass around large Coronas. What this country needed, Godsol firmly believed, was not a five-cent cigar but a dollar cigar and more men like himself to smoke them; a man who declined a cigar at eight o'clock in the morning belonged behind a ribbon counter, not in Godsol's employ. I used to try to save mine for my girl's old man but under Godsol's watchful eye it took considerable finesse to stick it in my vest pocket instead of my mouth. With this ritual over, he would briskly open the meetings. His first question to his Corona-punchy crew was invariably: "What's new, boys?" and without waiting for replies he would turn to Rodgers and ask, "What were the receipts in Des Moines yesterday?"; or to Grainger with, "What admission prices are charged at the Metropolitan, Washington?"; or to Dietz with some such jolt as, "What's the population of Hartford, Connecticut?" He always jotted

42

down our replies on small scraps of paper, a procedure guaranteed to send us all scurrying back to our offices to make sure we had given the correct answers.

On the other hand, I recall on one occasion passing a minor office in which one of the occupants, with two feet firmly planted on the desk, was staring somnolently out of the window. With alarm I noted that Godsol had also observed him. "Best man in the place," he commented. "Takes time off to think occasionally. I always distrust anybody who seems busy all the time."

After his own long hours at work, this superthyroid of the superman school would proceed to hit the high spots of Broadway's most luxurious gambling houses and speakeasies. He also used to travel from coast to coast in sovereign splendor, never occupying less than a dozen bedrooms, and always accompanied on his trips by some prominent, charming and hospitable actress. The dozen bedrooms puzzled me until I realized that the twosome was invariably attended by a retinue of valets, maids, secretaries, masseurs and other strange camp followers including Godsol's private bookie. When rumors of these trumpet-blared and neon-lighted liaisons leaked into, or leapt into, the newspaper gossip columns, he would accuse his entire publicity staff of neglecting its major assignment. This he regarded as killing detrimental true stories rather than circulating false ones, however helpful.

Occasionally he went home, not for such extraneous matters as slumber, solitude or sex, but to discuss business with Mrs. Godsol, who, with similar vigor, if less emotional intensity, conducted his Tecla-vending organization.

While still Chairman of the Board of Goldwyn Pictures, Godsol was instrumental in investing some of its and Du Pont's money in one of New York's early picture palaces, the Capitol Theatre, an establishment which was promoted and erected by Messmore Kendall, the noted architect and boulevardier. Its manager and showman was Major Edward Bowes. As a showman, Bowes' outstanding asset was his overwhelming confidence in Bowes. One of his ideas was that Aimee Semple McPherson, the evangelist, would prove a tremendous box-office attraction. He booked her for $5,000 a week and a split over $50,000, and promptly notified the police department to have a squad of police assigned to handle the anticipated opening day riot. The theatre's average weekly take was $40,000, but it dived to $17,500 with Aimee. *Variety* appraised her debut with the short comment, "She wears a white satin creation. Sexy but episcopalian."

When Godsol bought into the theatre he replaced Bowes with "Roxy" (*geboren* Rothapfel, anglicized to Rothafel), an appointment which irked the Major and the executive staff of the Capitol to such an extent that to placate all parties concerned, Bowes was elected vice-president of Goldwyn Pictures with no duties except to collect an additional salary of $25,000 a year. This was tough on the Goldwyn stockholders but motion picture investors have rarely been a pampered group.

Neither Kendall nor Bowes ever learned to love Roxy. In his book, *Never Let the Weather Interfere*, Kendall, with commendable restraint, says, "Roxy had a rare ability for personal advertising." The Capitol Theatre had inaugurated a radio broadcasting program for its own publicity purposes, but when Roxy came in he took it over lock, stock and microphone, christening it "Roxy and His Gang." Kendall further reports that "he was generous enough to make an occasional reference to the Capitol Theatre."

To the relief of all concerned, Roxy, in time, resigned to help promote a new palace. Its name to Roxy was not one of its lesser appeals: it was called the Roxy Theatre. In his pleas to potential stock buyers he promised to dedicate his talents to this monument for the rest of his life; a promise which he kept "only until he had an opportunity to go into something bigger," comments Mr. Kendall, therewith washing his hands of the whole subject of Roxy.

The "something bigger" was the new Radio City Music Hall which Roxy persuaded the Rockefellers to call Roxy's Music Hall. His personal office had a gold-plated ceiling. Before the first show opened he assured callers that it didn't make much difference who would be on the bill. As long as his name, Roxy, was featured, public acclaim was certain. The opening show was so colossal that it exhausted the customers: a 200-piece orchestra, a line of 150 girls, 100 singers and several hundred more assorted and stupendous performers. At the finale there were 500 people on the stage and less than a dozen die-hards in the auditorium. With a tradition of economy in their blood, the Rockefellers were speedily sated with supershowmanship and replaced Broadway's genius with a more efficient, if less colossal, management. The subsequent success of the Music Hall was largely due to the talents of Roxy's antipodal successors, quietly competent, self-effacing men like

Van Schmus, Eyssel and Downing, who eccentrically preferred to demonstrate their showmanship by the quality of the entertainment they sponsored rather than by the quantity of their personal publicity.

When Roxy took over the Capitol's radio broadcast one of the loudest critics of his ethics and loyalty was Bowes. After Roxy left, Bowes wasted no time in becoming the maestro of the mike and inaugurated the Amateur Hour, which soon became "The Major Bowes Amateur Hour," which soon became a national network program owned lock, stock, and microphone by Major Edward Bowes.

Godsol radiated charm, which he threw around in big gobs. When it failed to function he fell back on cash, which he distributed even more lavishly. When he paid his first call on Messmore Kendall, that tycoon was shocked to observe him surreptitiously slipping the butler a fifty-dollar bill. "What you think is intuition," Godsol would say to me, "is often only information—advance information." His huge Hispano-Suiza never waited in line to cross a ferry; ten-dollar bills passed to co-operative officials expedited its progress, and occasionally ten dollars was also handed to a startled car owner as Godsol's car shoved in front of his. I remember a party he once gave for a stockholder in Boston, a dignified old-school gentleman. The stockholder's invited friends were of the same, if not an older, school. At supper that night each of the ladies in the party found an envelope at her place containing ten crisp ten-dollar bills. The ladies seemed momentarily nonplused, but they kept their mementos.

Godsol invariably carried thousands of dollars loosely

crammed into every pocket of his pants, coat and overcoat. To watch him disrobe was to sit in the midst of a storm of greenbacks. "You never can tell when the banks may close," he used to say. His worries were justified. They did close—fourteen years later. His money-carrying propensity was, incidentally, in direct contrast to Goldwyn's. Sam, who prided himself on his svelte figure, never carried a wallet or a roll of bills on his person for fear of their bulge. When you traveled with Sam, you became his treasurer.

Godsol's main contribution to Goldwyn Pictures was to arrange for its obsequies. With Marcus Loew, who in addition to his theatre circuit had acquired Metro Pictures, Godsol in 1924 negotiated the merger which became Metro-Goldwyn-Mayer, launching Louis B. Mayer as its production head. After the merger Goldwyn formed a company of his own using the name Goldwyn. M-G-M promptly sued him on the grounds that it, not Goldwyn, owned the name. Fortunately for posterity, Goldwyn, sustained by the courts, declined to revert to Goldfish.

Also during his regime Godsol bought the picture rights to *Ben Hur* and sent June Mathis as scenarist, Charles Brabin as director, and George Walsh as star to Italy to produce it as the most stupendous, spectacular, de luxe film of all time. Handicapped both by adjectives and local authorities, not to mention Miss Mathis' conviction that her script was divinely inspired, they encountered all sorts of difficulties. They were later replaced with an even better second team—Carey Wilson, whom Miss Mathis regarded as the reincarnation of Rudyard Kipling; Fred Niblo and Ramon Novarro—but the newcomers encountered equal obstacles and eventually the whole outfit was transferred to Culver City by M-G-M where a bigger and better Circus Maximus was built and the most stupendous, spectacular, colossal film of all time was finally finished. M-G-M has continued to make it, under different titles, ever since, culminating, I suspect, in the present version of *Quo Vadis.*

Godsol's experiences with *Ben Hur* was not unlike that of Mutual Films, which back in 1914 assisted in financing the famous bandit Villa in one of his Mexican forays. In return for twenty-five thousand dollars Villa agreed to fight no battles except in daylight, and not until the Mutual cameras were properly placed to photograph what modern hand-to-hand fighting really looked like. Villa, in spite of his radical proclivities, was a strictly honorable citizen. In the face of frequent temptations, he consistently refused to fight until Mutual crews were strategically located to reproduce the combat. Wherever he went he was accompanied by the company's technicians bearing their heart-warming message, "Mutual Movies Make Time Fly."

When the negative was shipped back to the Mutual studios, however, it proved a great disappointment to the sedentary but bloodthirsty executives. If this was the last word in warfare Hollywood would have to do something about it. They shot most of the pictures all over again on a studio lot with an improved scenario and direction. To make it more realistic, scenes of far greater carnage were inserted. Thus, early in the history of the motion picture industry, the theory that the synthetic was preferable to the genuine was firmly established.

And it has continued ever since. Only recently, when

Paramount was shooting a sequence in *War of the Worlds*, a camera crew was sent to photograph the atomic blast near Las Vegas. On their return to Hollywood they screened the sequence and found it deeply disappointing. The blinding flash followed by the mushroom cloud rising over the desert was by no means spectacular enough for a modern science epic. The miniature experts in the special-effects department were summoned to meet the emergency and they proceeded to produce a visually much more thrilling explosion.

As Oscar Wilde or Groucho Marx or somebody once pointed out, nature has a habit of imitating art, and by the same token, movies have frequently served to instruct people in the customs attributed to them. For instance, when Edmund Grainger was producing the film *The Fabulous Texans*, he employed some Indians from a reservation to act as experts to see that the smoke signals called for by the script were thoroughly authentic. On the completion of the picture, Grainger warmly congratulated them on their fine supervision. "It was easy," one of the Indians answered. "We learned how to do it from the movies."

Another similar incident occurred a few years ago when the representatives of M-G-M arrived in the Belgian Congo to arrange for the screening of *King Solomon's Mines*. They were distressed to discover that the tall Watusi tribesmen were quite hep. They wore sports shirts and tennis shoes and plastered their hair down like city slickers. Hasty long-distance conferences with Hollywood ensued and eventually two hundred wigs with the proper African hair-do were rapidly manufactured and shipped by plane to the ultra-civilized natives.

It is also rumored that when the late beloved Robert Flaherty made his memorable *Nanook of the North* he found the benighted Canadian Eskimos quite ignorant of how to make their igloos or how to fish through ice. Fortunately Flaherty, who knew everything (and always modestly denied the story), was able to instruct them in these primitive arts. The first version of *Nanook*, by the way, was completely destroyed by fire. On this, as on many subsequent occasions, the indomitable Flaherty took disaster in his stride, and promptly returned for a second year to the frozen North and reshot the entire picture. He said the fire was a blessing: he made a far better picture the second time.

The results of an ingenious invention as far back as 1897 by one Edward Amet also testified to the superiority of the ersatz article over the actual. He reproduced the Battle of Santiago in a bathtub. Working in miniature he constructed in detail the ships and armament of both the Americans and Spaniards. With electrically controlled devices he manipulated boats, waves, guns and smoke effects. The ensuing battle was alleged to have been shot with a telescopic lens on a craft far removed from the scene of action. It was generally accepted as authentic and a print was even purchased by the Spanish government for its military archives.

The Godsol-M-G-M *Ben Hur* was not the first film version of that famous story to prove unnecessarily costly. In December, 1907, a one-reel version was produced by one of the earliest companies, Kalem. It was heralded in its advertising as "positively the most superb and costly moving picture spectacle ever made in America," and its superlatives were justified, for although Kalem expended little for sets or actors it neglected to obtain the motion picture rights and was sued by the estate of the author, Lew Wallace. This action was the first of its kind in movie history and Kalem, searching for an out, replied that it had produced "merely a series of photographs," and that actually it ought to be rewarded for advertising the book so efficiently. A hardhearted court was not impressed by this defense and eventually Kalem had to pay twenty-five thousand dollars, establishing a precedent in legal rights and advertising accuracy.

In addition to Godsol's investment in the Capitol Theatre he acquired interests in other theatres in various parts of the country. These investments were not altogether evidences of his lavish way with money. He was merely trying to keep up with some of the bigger boys in the industry who were already engaged in solidifying their production and distribution activities by invading the field of exhibition. Handicapped in the battle for theatres by inadequate resources as compared to such moguls as Zukor or Fox, Godsol could only pick up some of the crumbs they had overlooked. One of these crumbs, in every sense of the word, was a group of theatres in and around Chicago, which was owned by Nate Ascher and his associates.

After I had worked for some months as his confidential secretary, Godsol summoned me into his office one day. "The trouble with you, Arthur," he said, "is that you don't know how to write decent English. I need somebody with a good education. Get me a college boy who knows that a business letter starts 'Yours of the 10th inst. to hand and in reply beg to state.' As for you, take the next train to Chicago. We're losing our shirt with Ascher but maybe you can help save the tail."

· IV ·

My chores in connection with the Capitol Theatre had been so menial and my acquaintance with its operation so limited that Nate Ascher and his associates constituted, in 1921, my actual introduction to the world of big-city showmen. Until then, I had rubbed elbows only with the cowpath and whistle-stop exhibitors of my salesman days, and, in more ways than geographically, Ascher's world was far removed from theirs.

For one thing, my new associates spoke a foreign language. When upon my arrival Ascher told me he had been advised to "take a bath," I agreed that it was a good thing to do occasionally, not realizing that I was encouraging him to go into bankruptcy. As things turned out, I never gave a sager piece of advice. When shortly thereafter the manager of one of the theatres told me he had decided to cut out "ten-percenters" and rely more on "pluggers," I heartily endorsed his decision, assuming that pluggers were reliable, hard-working men and women. He accordingly replaced theatrical agency talent with singers who were furnished free of charge by the music publishing houses to plug their new songs.

By degrees I learned that a "gridiron" was not a football field but a rigging loft above the stage from which curtains and drapes were hung; that the "colonial clap" was not a pioneer social disease but an audience's method of audibly expressing its disapproval; that a "turtle" was not a slow-moving animal but an actor out of work and that a "grind," in addition to being a lascivious dance, was also a theatre featuring continuous performances. I further ascertained that "flesh" meant vaudeville acts and that the policy of most of the Ascher theatres was strictly screen entertainment except for week-ends, or, as Nate put it, "No flesh until Saturday night."

Ascher himself was completely unacquainted with any records except those of his bookie, but an ingenious bookkeeper, unbeknownst to him, had installed a triple-entry system. One set of records, designed for bankers and inquiring creditors, indicated splendid results. A second, intended for picture distributors, showed business to be so miserable that it brought tears to the eyes of the hardest-boiled salesmen and justified requests for reduced film rentals. A third set was devised to give harassed auditors an inkling of the actual, if tangled, financial affairs of the concern. It was after partially mastering these intricacies that I wired Godsol "Aschers to ashes," which confirmed his low estimate of my talents as a correspondent. When he was passing through Chicago en route to the Coast a little later I persuaded him to look at the books himself. After studying them for half an hour, he shook his head and said, "There's only one thing I understand about these balance sheets. The liabilities are good."

Ascher had recently constructed in the Loop one of its early picture palaces, the Roosevelt. It did not compare in size or in synthetic splendor with its neighbor, the Chicago, erected by Balaban & Katz, but it gave him the great asset of a first-run house; that is, a theatre which plays pictures ahead of all others in the community. This, in addition to prestige, created greater purchasing power with the distributors. He had also acquired first-run houses in Dayton, Cincinnati, Milwaukee, Manitowoc, Wisconsin, and other thriving communities, and twenty neighborhood houses in Chicago. With such a nucleus, profits should have been substantial. Unfortunately, Ascher had expanded too rapidly, and had neither the organization nor the executive capacity to organize and operate a large and growing circuit. He had had the acumen to rush into movie exhibition in its initial days when it was close to impossible not to make profits, and he had also been sufficiently aggressive to acquire a number of well-located theatres while they were still inexpensive. Ascher attributed these early successes to the genius of Ascher. When everything began to crumble around him he still maintained his impregnable faith in Ascher.

Outwardly hale, hearty and a backslapper, he had no affection for any backs he slapped unless they were feminine and responsive. Superficially shrewd, he had no real understanding or comprehension of the potentialities of the exhibition business, but under the impression that he was himself a two-fisted, hard-boiled fighter, he folded like a Japanese lantern when he found himself up against some of the really tough gangster racketeers of the early twenties.

The house managers were underpaid and to make both ends meet a few of them also availed themselves of a little "honest graft." A favorite method by which this was accomplished was through "palming" tickets. With the connivance of his cashier, a manager, with comparative safety, could pick up the stubs of incoming patrons and, instead of dropping them into the ticket box, return them to the cashier to be resold, this time for the benefit of his own pocket. On the other hand most of the managers were surprisingly faithful and conscientious. One of them, as he was closing his theatre one night, was attacked by three gangsters, who trussed him up and toasted his toes, but he stoically refused to reveal the safe's combination. A few nights later they returned properly equipped and carted the whole safe away.

With revenue spilling through so many chinks and crevices, and urged on by the shirt-losing Godsol, I became his Dutch boy holding the dikes with all fingers and toes. Next to a thorough knowledge of an industry, unadulterated ignorance is the surest road to success. I assembled all of the Ascher house managers and assured them I was a firm exponent of personal initiative and free enterprise; that we were facing an emergency which I believed could be dealt with by reverting to the principles of individual

"There's only one thing I understand—the liabilities are good."

rather than circuit theatre operation, and that thereafter they were to take over the control of their theatres. My words were met with a spontaneous lethargy, but I kept going. They were to sit in with the booker and decide themselves what pictures they wanted and what days to play them. They were to select their own vaudeville acts and lay out their own advertising. Over Ascher's outraged protests I wound up by putting them all on a profit-sharing basis—and hurriedly ducked.

Business, however, responded promptly to the new morale of increased responsibility and better remuneration and I was gratified to be told later by one manager that he had found it, surprisingly enough, almost as lucrative to run his theatre honestly as dishonestly. As a result of this elementary experiment I tried for twenty years to persuade other theatre circuits to create managerial bonuses —with no success. A Paramount-Publix executive, for instance, told me the cost would be excessive. When his great company eventually went into bankruptcy it was disclosed that for several years four of its major executives had been dividing annual bonuses of approximately two million dollars.

To help me in my new enterprise, Godsol sent Roxy to Chicago to give me in two days the benefit of his years of experience and wisdom in showmanship. My first lesson came when I met him at the railroad station in my battered Ford. He gave it one withering glance, hastened to a phone and rented a Packard limousine and chauffeur. "How can anyone believe you are important," he said, "if you don't act and look important?"

Correctly encased, he then proceeded to visit all of the Ascher houses in the manner of a plumed and white-gloved admiral inspecting his fleet. After the grand tour and back at his three-room suite at the Drake he sent me out to buy a box of colored crayons and some large sheets of drawing paper. With these, in vermilion, violet and Kelly green, he sketched his ideas of how the front of every Ascher theatre should be redecorated and how their canopies should be reconstructed; they should be made so distinctive, he advised, that even the least observant passer-by would know that he was in the presence of an Ascher house.

It was my belief that passers-by for blocks around would think they were in the presence of the aurora borealis but I told him I thought his ideas were beautiful, I wished I could use them, but that my major perplexity was how to meet the weekly payroll and film bills, and did he have any ideas on those subjects? The question was so boorish he did not deign to answer it.

His next proposal was that all of our houses, even the smallest, should be operated on a de luxe basis. The major difference between a de luxe and any other movie show consists of closing the curtains after the feature film, reopening them for the shorts, closing them again and reopening them for the news. This suggestion also left me cold for crass commercial considerations which I tried to explain. A strongly entrenched operators' union exacted a twenty-dollar-a-week higher wage scale per man for the hocus-pocus of sliding curtains; also, in the theatres where we had curtains they were too moth-eaten, I felt, to stand the de luxe trips.

Back in New York Roxy reported to Joe Godsol that I lacked even the basic elements of a good showman and that I should be promptly returned to my banker patron, for whom—if I proved honest—I might make a passable cashier.

Roxy's trip to Chicago, however, was not, for him or me, altogether fruitless. Waiting for the Century, he observed to me that there was no eye-arresting display to distinguish this crack train from its less potent rivals. Upon his return to New York he advised the management that a red carpet spread from the gate to the Pullmans would indicate the Century's pre-eminence in the field of luxury and service. The New York Central's executives were greatly impressed by this suggestion from so distinguished an impresario. They accepted it and rewarded him with an annual pass, and to this day the red carpet is still unrolled twice a day in New York by eight workmen. Every time I step on it I feel a tingle of pride in having had such a hand—even vicarious—in history in the making.

Shortly after Roxy's visit I played another and equally important role in the making of history. In those strenuous times freak endurance contests flourished. Competitive couples danced in marathons until the men collapsed (the women usually were still going strong); bicycle riders entered six-day contests and rode until exhausted, and an early breed of isolationists was in long-term residence on the tops of all available steeples and flagpoles. In keeping with this popular trend I decided that a long-distance organ-playing contest would stimulate business. Business needed to be particularly stimulated in Manitowoc. Owing to a series of Hollywood scandals—Wallace Reid and his dope, the Fatty Arbuckle case, and the murder of William Desmond Taylor and the rumored connections with it of Mabel Normand and Mary Miles Minter—a Purity League had sprung up in Manitowoc and was strongly urging its citizens to renounce their movie dalliance and return to their churches. Accordingly I decided that the Manitowoc organist should be crowned the national champion. Plans were formulated that other organists in Cincinnati, Dayton, Chicago and elsewhere would one by one withdraw from the grueling contest, whereupon we would wire to Manitowoc that its local man was the victor and with newsreel cameras clicking and newspapers seeking interviews he would be borne in triumph from his bench, the "Shipwreck Kelly of the console."

For a series of uninteresting reasons the contest was called off at the last minute. I notified all of the organists of the change but unfortunately we overlooked the main one in Manitowoc. If any historian is interested, there was an organist in that town who played for fifty-eight solid hours, which was, still is and I think will forever be the all-time record. We gave him an impressive plaque to commemorate his achievement. It was inadequate acclaim, I still shamefacedly feel, for so great and true a champion. He did little, however, to stimulate business.

Major Bowes also spent a day with me in Chicago en route to the Coast. It was at a time when I had just discovered that an Ascher executive, in cahoots with some unscrupulous film salesman, had put into operation a nefarious little scheme by which pictures were charged to the company at considerably more than the price agreed upon, and he and his confederates shared in the gravy. I was sufficiently naïve to tell Bowes about this before advising New York, and the Major, as soon as he was out of my presence, wired Godsol, "It took me only a few hours in Chicago to uncover a plot to swindle us. Unable to stay here longer but have cautioned Mayer and advised him how to proceed."

A notorious South Side café was our after-office-hours office and every night after twelve we gathered there with the house managers who reported their receipts for the day and discussed our plans for the future. The café was also the scene of our social life and in our nightly rendezvous I, too, in time, acquired a few personal friends among its distinguished racketeer clientele. On one occasion I discovered that our payrolls were being padded by another of our light-fingered executives. I promptly discharged him and the following day a character right out of one of our gangster movies called on me and told me what happened in Chicago to people who didn't play right. I reported his visit to my South Side playmates. In those days the list price for bumping off a not too prominent offender was five thousand dollars. They offered to do it for me wholesale. After a few drinks they insisted on doing it for nothing. With some difficulty I tempered their enthusiasm and limited their co-operation to a visit to my ex-executive, who was warned that anything that happened to me could happen to him also. I had no more callers but for many months I had dreams of sinking into Lake Michigan clad in a cement vest.

For most of the men with whom I have been associated I have, in spite of differences in taste and tactics, developed some sort of admiration and respect. Maybe I was still young and overcritical, or maybe the nature of my association with Nate Ascher was such that we could not be friends; maybe I didn't try hard enough. Maybe I just plain didn't like him. I owe him, however, one great debt. He introduced me to Sam Katz and the Balabans.

· V ·

SAM KATZ'S FATHER was a refugee from Russian oppression whose dream in life was that his son might grow up to be a concert pianist. Although he made a meager living as a barber, he had, with many sacrifices, seen to it that from the age of eight, Sam had taken "classical" piano lessons every single week. At the age of thirteen when Sam broke the news to his parents that he had found a job playing piano in a small West Side Chicago movie theatre, his mother broke down and wept and his father wailed in disgrace, "It's worse than playing in a bawdy house." When Sam pointed out, with pride, that he had wangled eight dollars a week for the job—a dollar more than the previous player had been getting—his father was not impressed. Sam was.

By the time he graduated from high school, he had acquired three theatres and was making a profit of four hundred dollars a week. If this seems unbelievable, it should be pointed out perhaps that in those days a theatre could be bought for a few hundred dollars in cash and a promissory note for the balance. In 1907, and at only sixteen, he was already a self-made man who not only admired his maker but had a profound faith in him (a faith which in the years to come was frequently, if not invariably, justified). But in spite of his prosperity he said to a friend at this period in his life, "I see no future in this business for me. What I intend to do is study law as a profession." And this he did for the next two years, operating his theatres on the side—undoubtedly the best self-heeled law student ever to open a volume of Blackstone—until he was swept off his heels and out of the legal profession one night by the sight of Sarah Bernhardt in *Queen Elizabeth*.

Seen today, this famous French production, the first four-reeler (approximately forty minutes) ever to be distributed in the United States, is nothing to rave about. It was directed, photographed and acted as if stage technique could be transplanted intact to the screen. The camera stayed respectfully at a distance from the aging star and little of her perfect artistry is revealed. The divine Sarah said about it, "This is my guarantee of immortality." Fortunately her fame is more securely established. (Her leading man in the picture was Lou Tellegen, who later became the author of a confessional called *Women Have Been Kind to Me* which earned him the sobriquet of Cad, and Kiss and Tellegen.) With Sam, however, the picture was love at first sight. He knew that no other career could ever be as exciting or as profitable as operating theatres where such marvels could be shown to millions of people.

Abe and Barney Balaban were two of a family of ten children born back of their father's little grocery and fish market. They were reared in an atmosphere of sour pickles, herring and love. Abe's first job in Chicago was in a circus; he yanked nails out of old planks, earned twenty-five cents an hour, saw the show free and never got show business out of his system. He next became an errand boy for a tailoring firm by day but by night he began to spend his time singing for pennies, first in all-night cafés and dives, and then graduating to the nickelodeons where he vocalized repulsively illustrated song slides. He quickly noticed that the theatres where he sang prospered and that there were never any complaints except that the shows were too short. At family conferences he repeatedly pointed out the advantage of movies over bologna until Mama Balaban finally agreed. "Think of it," she sighed, "a cash business with no stock of fish or vegetables to spoil." Barney, who worked for a cold-storage company, also succumbed in a short time and the two brothers pooled their savings of $178.00 and rented a shooting gallery at Twelfth Street and Kedzie Avenue. Operating the Kedzie in the evenings, Abe continued to carry cloth to pants makers all day and Barney to work at his cold-storage job. In the tradition of family-run theatres, sister Ida played the piano and brother Max sold tickets. When he was not too busy getting in and out of financial emergencies and helping Mama Balaban look after the younger children, Papa Balaban acted as the janitor.

Business at the Kedzie was good. It rose from a first week of $88.75 to $200 the following, but shortly rumors were afloat that competitors were looking for "locations" on their street. Alarmed, the boys sought the help of Judge Wallace, a sixty-five-year-old strict Scotch Presbyterian gentleman with whom Barney had only a nodding acquaintance. Even that early in his career, however, Barney's transparent integrity and keen business judgment were so apparent that the Judge loaned him twenty-five thousand dollars. Over the years these same qualities in Barney have impressed such hard-headed financiers as the Rosenwalds, John Hertz and S. W. Strauss to the tune of millions. They were never the losers.

With the loan the Balabans bought their own theatre, the Circle, and in it they settled down and began to develop a new type of operation. At the Kedzie, Abe had already toyed with a novel idea which has since become known as "presentations." On St. Patrick's Day he ran a picture called *The Irish Blacksmith*. In convincing make-up he billed himself as Timmy Mahoney, The Irish Lark, and sang in conjunction with it "My Wild Irish Rose," "Mother Machree" and "Ireland Must Be Heaven for My Mother Came from There." There wasn't a dry eye in the house. The Circle, however, was located in a strictly Jewish neighborhood and with the move Abe had to make some restrictive and concessionary changes in his repertoire. He continued with such couplings as "I'm Afraid to Go Home in the Dark" sung with Maurice Costello's *The Evil Men Do*, but his most popular numbers were "Nathan, Nathan, Tell Me Vot Are You Vaiting For," "Put It On,

67

Take It Off, Wrap It Up, Take It Home," and "Cohen Owed Me Ninety-seven Dollars." To these solo renditions he added volume and impressiveness by backing himself up with a male quartet costumed in baggy pants and size nine derbies. His clientele was delighted with the act.

In the face of more prosaic problems the boys showed equal competence. There was the small but troublesome one of free admission for children up to the age of seven. Every child in the neighborhood claimed to be eligible. Young Dave Balaban, then only fourteen himself, solved this one. Regardless of what nature had done to the material at hand, he decided, himself, how tall a seven-year-old should be, put a chalk mark on the wall indicating his decree, and the kids were backed up to it. Under the line they went in free. Abe instituted a service by which sleeping babies were left in tagged baby buggies on the sidewalk while the mothers went inside to enjoy the show. If the baby cried during the performance a slide would be flashed on the screen, "Mother Number 47, your baby is crying." And in the handling of the finances, Barney showed an early aptitude which clearly explains his current well-deserved reputation as being the most businesslike and economy-minded man in the industry.

Sam Katz and the Balabans met, merged and as Balaban & Katz blossomed into the greatest innovators in the history of motion picture exhibition.

Their first big venture was Chicago's Central Park, which they erected in 1917. This twenty-four-hundred-seater was the Middle West's first, if not—in the strictest sense of the words—America's first, "Picture Palace."

To these solo renditions Abe added volume and impressiveness by backing himself up with a male quartet in baggy pants and size 9 derbies.

When the New York Strand was erected in 1913 and the Rialto in 1915, both had been acclaimed palaces of matchless beauty and comfort. The Central Park with its twenty-four hundred seats outpalaced and outcomforted them. And it was soon surpassed by their succeeding projects, the Chicago, the Riviera, the Tivoli and the Uptown.

Starting with the Central Park, at a time when hotel, restaurant and railroad executives ridiculed the idea, they installed air conditioning; they sacrificed seating capacity for plenty of leg room and perfect sight lines, and they experimented with every variety of newfangled plush upholstered seat until they developed a chair so constructed and tilted that it was a pleasure to relax in it through even the dullest pictures. Waiting crowds in the lobby were kept from getting restive with music, coffee, cake and chewing gum; artists made sketches of them which they received free; models showed the latest styles and tea readers told fortunes. "The wonder," as *Variety* has since suggested, "was that any of the patrons cared about getting past the lobby."

They equipped the playroom of their Riviera Theatre with a sandbox, slides, seesaws, and suitable toys with trained attendants to supervise the youngsters while their mothers relaxed at the show. And their unerring instinct made it apparent to them that men who worked hard all day in subordinate capacities and women escaping for a few hours from the bondage of stoves and diapers would appreciate not only surroundings which surpassed their wildest dreams of luxury and gilded glamour but an environment in which they, themselves, might for a change be subordinated to. A West Point captain was cajoled from the Army to instill military discipline and precision into the ushers. "The patron is our guest" was the rule and nowhere were guests treated with such deference. Roxy had told me that tipping could never be abolished, but no Balaban & Katz employee would have dreamed of accepting a tip for any of his many courtesies.

It must be admitted, however, that Balaban & Katz were responsible not only for the unprecedented comforts of the modern picture theatre but for many of its artistic atrocities. The repulsive splendor of rococo decorations, gargantuan crystal chandeliers, fake Doric columns and cathedral windows looking out on nothing, sinking carpets, rising pipe organs and overzealous, gold-braided service staffs were all theirs and they were quickly and widely copied all over the country with even greater pomp, less taste—and similar profits.

Abe was the introducer of "gigantic presentations." When Valentino's *Blood and Sand* played the Balaban & Katz houses, it was presented with sunlit patios and Spanish singers, dancers and guitar players. With Clara Bow's *It* (so called because Walter Wanger once heard Elinor Glyn say, "That girl has it"), Abe came through with a hot jazz band and a not so hot version of a youthful petting party with more singing and dancing than insidious sex. When he played *Humoresque*, he interrupted the picture to bring a young violinist onto the stage to exemplify the picture's theme of a boy artist encouraged to practice by his adoring mother. He spent thousands of dollars on name acts: John Philip Sousa (for Fourth of July patriotic music),

Eddie Cantor, Ruby Keeler, Paul Whiteman, the Marx Brothers, Ruth Etting, Sophie Tucker and all of the other luminaries of the time, as well as many who were to be the luminaries of the future. And with Paul Ash wielding the baton and wiggling his well-developed hips at the Oriental, Abe was the Edison of the master-of-ceremonies idea and "Give the little girl a great big hand."

Barney and Sam meantime gathered around themselves in executive capacities the ablest young men they could find. To head their advertising department they hired William Hollander, formerly the motion picture editor of the Chicago *Daily News* and today the outstanding veteran in the field of theatre advertising. Hollander was assisted by Lloyd Lewis, who was to become the author of delightful and authoritative books about Lincoln, Grant and Sherman. Also Oscar Doob, now one of the leading executives of Loew's theatres; William Pine, who with William Thomas became the most successful producer of B pictures in Hollywood; Ben Serkowich, the celebrated exploiter; Les Kaufman, later of the producing firm of Fanchon & Marco, and a score of others.

Their first office boy was David Lipton, today head of Universal's advertising department and one of the most capable publicists in the industry. At the age of thirteen he heard that the owners of the new Central Park Theatre wanted an office boy and he decided to favor them with his services. Three hundred other lads had the same idea and stormed the B & K office. After days of weeding, the list was reduced to two, one of them David. He was interviewed by everyone in the place and eventually passed on for final inspection to Sam Katz. For an hour Katz questioned him: What education did he have? What was his home life like? Was he in good health? What illnesses had he had? Did he save? What did he expect to acquire in life? Had he any consciousness of any particular ambition? What were his hobbies? In recalling the interview David told me he thought that he must have been mistaken about the nature of the position; the uneasy feeling came over him that he was being interviewed for no office boy's job but for Woodrow Wilson's.

David was the eventual winner and he was advised that his salary would be thirteen dollars a week. He protested that thirteen was an unlucky number for him but that fourteen wasn't. It took two more days of interviews before the matter was settled with the hair-splitting compromise of thirteen-fifty and a promise of a fifty-cent raise if he made good.

With all of the attention devoted to the cross examination and hiring of this, their first office boy, one basic factor was overlooked by the partners. Being under age, David had no working papers and every time an inspector came around he had to waste the company's time hiding in a closet.

In the handling of this minor problem, however, Katz displayed the minute attention to detail and the emphasis on skilled personnel which was later to reach full bloom in his mammoth effort to put "show biz" on a highly organized and businesslike basis.

Not long after his acquisition of Ascher's Roosevelt Theatre, Sam heard a rumor that I was promoting the erection of a new theatre in the Loop, hoping that he would surely buy it rather than have it fall into the hands of some competitive operator. Such chicanery, which at that early stage in my career would never have occurred to me, made him regard me as a man to keep an eye on. He further attributed to me the improved results in the Ascher theatres for which the managerial bonuses and emancipation from home office dictation were entirely responsible. I had also created a mild sensation in local movie circles by twice paying distributors more than my contracts specified, when their pictures did far better business than anticipated. This was a startling innovation in trade practices and it proved thoroughly unsuccessful as it was based on my false assumption that the distributors would treat me equally generously when the situation was reversed. Having made up his mind that I should be watched, however, and acting on the well-established movie tradition that "If he's an s.o.b. he had better be *my* s.o.b.," Katz offered me a job in his organization.

When I joined Balaban & Katz in the middle twenties, they had just acquired a 50 per cent interest in the firm of Lubliner & Trinz, then owners of the leading Chicago neighborhood house circuit. After prolonged debate, they had to leave its name unchanged because no theatre marquee could be devised large enough to permit the names of Balaban, Katz, Lubliner & Trinz to appear on it. My first assignment was to represent B & K in the operation of this circuit.

The frictions within Lubliner & Trinz were much as though the Montagues and the Capulets had gone into business together. The firm had twenty-four theatres, and at the time I appeared on the scene was just purchasing a twenty-fifth. This created a serious impasse as twelve houses were managed by Lubliner relatives and twelve by Trinz relatives. The balance of power was in jeopardy. I suggested disposing of a losing theatre but this was heresy. Theatres are to ambitious circuit owners like heirlooms to ancient families—symbols of prestige to be sacrificed only in desperate emergencies. Eventually we acquired a thoroughly undesirable twenty-sixth shooting gallery, sent a hurried call to an equally undesirable relative in distant parts and restored peace and maintained equality in the company's inner councils.

Lubliner & Trinz were specialists in costless advertising. We never took big newspaper ads or used billboards, but merchandised our pictures through any channel which did not require an outlay of cash. We promoted ice cream for distribution on hot days, and generously tossed out prizes donated by local merchants to patrons who guessed the correct temperature on cold days. We gave away dishes, had country store nights, spelling bees, paper caps and clubs with buttons and membership cards. We placed our faith more on these frills than on our features.

We made local movies in which our customers could see themselves acting. We produced our own Chicago newsreels and we conducted every imaginable kind of contest on our stage, from the most freckled kids to the most beautiful legs—won by a nice lady of seventy.

When we played *Love Comes Along*, we anticipated the antics of television by many years and inserted a small notice in the Want Ads reading, "Wanted, a young couple to get married. We will furnish the trousseau and pay expenses." We then promoted from neighborhood merchants much more expensive gifts than the bride and groom would have received had they been married at home. Flowers were furnished by the local florist, and the happy couple was married on the stage with heart-warming results for the box office, if not for their future happiness. For *The Saturday Night Kid*, we had girls with intriguing voices call men on the phone to try to make dates with them for Saturday night at the theatre. When we played *The Old Homestead* we had a pie-baking contest with appreciative newspaper reporters as the judges. For *Sherlock Holmes* we conducted a treasure hunt with some impressive imitation pearls hidden on top of a telegraph pole, and colored direction cards indicating to the hunters if the trail was growing hotter or colder. To exploit *Human Wreckage* we borrowed twenty-five thousand dollars' worth of drugs from a trustful wholesale chemical house and had two policemen assigned to guard the lobby display night and day. And for *The Covered Wagon* the ushers wore coonskin caps and between their ushering chores marched around the block.

When *The Covered Wagon* was being made, incidentally, around 1922 or '23, Jesse Lasky, who was making it, told me he received a wire from his boss, Adolph Zukor, advising him to discontinue work on it as exhibitors were complaining that too many Westerns were being made. Lasky wired back, "Wagon not a Western. It is an epic." To this he received the reply, "In view of fact it is an epic and not a Western, kindly proceed without further delay."

I worked amicably for about three years with Lubliner & Trinz until I found one of the Trinz retainers confusing the company's finances with his own. This discovery on my part strangely infuriated the head of the clan not at the culprit but at me. I arrived one morning to find my office door barricaded. I threatened to smash it in and Trinz threatened to throw me out of the twenty-first-story window. He stood over six feet, weighed two hundred pounds and, although advanced in years, seemed better equipped than I to implement any threats. Only the intervention of his partner, Harry Lubliner, prevented actual violence.

Except in the presence of a Trinz, Lubliner was the most pacific character I ever met next to Ferdinand the Bull. And, like Ferdinand, he was a flower lover. He had been a street flower vendor before getting into the theatre business and his first love had apparently stayed with him as his office was always filled with roses or delphinium. He was soft-spoken in an industry where it is the practice to shout and pound a desk with or without provocation. He, on the contrary, would say, hesitantly, "Would you mind if I express an opinion?" He always knocked courteously before entering an office. Six nights a week he went home and to bed by nine but on Saturday nights he went to hell in a big way. He played pinochle with relatives until midnight and was known to drink as many as two bottles of beer. Although peaceful and retiring generally, when irked by a Trinz he could become forceful and intimidating. He was aglow with fighting fervor on the day he stepped between Trinz and me.

The cause of the fracas was present throughout and remained coolly disinterested. He found a more lucrative job and a few months later told me he had decided honesty was the best policy. He had tried both.

After this unfortunate incident my relations with Trinz remained strained. Never again did he ask me to share his luncheons with him, the first course of which consisted of caviar served in a huge soup tureen. (When he drank champagne, it was out of a seidel.) No longer did I enjoy the privilege of receiving tips on his horses, which invariably ran last. I was not invited to ride with him again in his gargantuan custom-made Cunningham, a number which was a copy of one owned by Al Reeves, the burlesque magnate, which was once described in *Variety* as "a limousine built along the lines of a Queen Anne cottage with latticed windows and containing everything except a tennis court in the front yard."

In it, Trinz used to inspect the theatres always in strict alphabetical rather than geographical sequence. Word of his coming would be wafted abroad and no manager, however lazy or inefficient, failed to have adequate warning to get his lobby clean, his exits clear, the bulbs of his house lights all working, and himself fortuitously near the entrance, hard at work.

One of the Lubliner & Trinz houses was the Biograph, the theatre patronized by and in front of which John Dillinger was shot dead. Although the historic incident took place almost a decade after I had left Lubliner & Trinz and Chicago behind, for the benefit of historians I can report that the picture Dillinger saw that Sunday night was

78

Manhattan Melodrama. (I picked up this item listening to a recent radio quiz show.)

My own inspection methods of the theatres were less predictable than Trinz's and consequently less popular. The practice of arriving unexpectedly and strolling in unobserved to see how the theatre was actually operated was regarded as clearly subversive.

In one case where I was suspicious that the manager and the cashier were in collusion and palming tickets, I hired a detective agency to check the house. I also continued personally to observe it. My first report from the private eye started: "Believe we have already spotted outside contact. Suspicious-looking middle-aged man slipped in rear exit, seemed more interested in behavior of ushers and patrons than in show and before departure was closeted for some time in animated conversation with manager."

What I resented mainly was the epithet "middle-aged." I was in my early thirties and still under the blissful misconception that I was a dashing young man about town.

· VI ·

AFTER THE TRINZ EPISODE, in the interests of amity, if not efficiency, it was decided that I should transfer my baleful activities to another circuit in which Balaban & Katz had an interest, the Great States Theatres. This was a mushroom growth which was rapidly spreading all over Illinois. Its meteoric rise was due to the unquenchable energy of its chief, Jules (Jay) Rubens, whose career and character are highly representative of the early days of theatre acquisition "by persuasion if possible, or by harsher methods if necessary," as the saying used to go.

Circuit building began when the industry was still in its diapers. It started one day when it occurred to some theatre owner, no doubt while counting the day's take, that since patrons would pay to see a picture in one theatre, the receipts from several theatres would be proportionately sweeter provided, of course, that he, himself, owned those several theatres. Thoughts of this type are not, by nature, local. All over the country the grabbing of theatres suddenly began and spread with gold rush fervor, resulting in one of the most concrete demonstrations in the history of American business enterprise that big fish eat up little fish and are in turn eaten up by bigger ones.

At the time of my switch to Jay Rubens there were about twelve thousand movie theatres throughout the country. Approximately a fourth of them were already organized into smaller circuits and most of these were in transit into the maws of the larger circuits, just as Rubens' Great States and Lubliner & Trinz had already succumbed, in part—as had others—to the up-and-coming Balaban & Katz.

In New England aggressive operators like Al Black, Bill Gray and Nate Gordon were consolidating their consolidations. In Louisiana, the rising kingfish were not only Huey Long but the more enduring E. V. Richards of the Saenger Amusement Co. Also in the South, representatives of rival theatrical groups were sweeping their way from North Carolina to Texas with aggressive "wrecking crews" and "dynamite squads," so called because of the methods ascribed to them by apprehensive if not always entirely accurate witnesses.

One was to drop a few stink bombs in the auditoriums of exhibitors who were so unreasonable as to wish to stay in business for themselves. This procedure was calculated to discourage attendance by even the most insensitive of patrons and encouraged exhibitors to be more amenable to the terms offered by Lynch. Other charges, strongly if not always convincingly denied by Lynch, were "accidental" explosions and fires in booths and houses, and inexplicable injuries to the persons of stubborn individualists who did not know what was best for them. If you believed all you heard, some of these Southern marches made Sherman's look like a cadet drill.

In the Middle West, where I was an eyewitness, the Fitzpatrick & McElroy circuit had expanded by peaceful if not entirely kindly methods, and was, in turn, being eyed by Great States. One of the theatres in this group was the one in which I had been offered a half interest back in my salesman days if I would marry the owner's daughter. She had, by this time, acquired a husband. The fact that every circuit was trying to get theatres in any way possible, and that her new husband happened to be a Fitzpatrick & McElroy lieutenant were coincidences which I banished from my mind. With lead-pipe gallantry, I clung to the belief that he had found charms in her which I had been incapable of appreciating.

Another and far more important Midwest circuit expanding rapidly at the time through Minnesota and the Dakotas (and which was also destined for consolidation with even bigger operators) was Rubin & Finkelstein. In his early pioneer days Rubin, Sr. (his son Eddie is now a prominent Northwest exhibitor), worked out a unique system for the highly desired fast turnover in the movie business, a need commonly known as "gettem in, gettem out." His system started accidentally. In a rural community where he had just opened one of his converted stores, he put an exit sign over its back door, primarily and innocently to show his patrons the way out. His clientele, however, many of whom could not read English, paid no attention to it and continued to leave by the front door. To clarify and expedite matters Mr. Rubin began to stand by the back door and occasionally to say, "This way out." He noticed that if he said, "This way out," when his rube customers were just coming in, they thought he meant for them to keep going.

He did not feel called upon to discourage this interpretation. Indeed, an usher was hired with no duties other than to stand at the rear and say, "This way out," every time a customer showed up at the front. The result was that half of the little community was under the impression that the standard procedure in a movie theatre was to pay your money at the box office and look at the flickers as you walked down the aisle and out the back door.

At a later date, his partner, Finkelstein (whose son Harold is also a currently well known exhibitor), showed equal talent in dealing with city slickers. One from New York by the name of Sam Goldwyn once called on the firm in its Minneapolis headquarters to take him to task for not buying more Goldwyn pictures. As was frequently the case when Sam personally discussed with exhibitors the rentals he wanted for his pictures as compared with the rentals they were prepared to pay, the visit turned into a brawl. At its height Sam pounded the table and proclaimed for all the world to hear that he would build his own theatre in Minneapolis and run Rubin & Finkelstein out of business. Mr. Finkelstein reached for his hat. "Come with me," he calmly suggested, "and I'll show you the best sites."

Jay Rubens was the epitome of all of the virtues and some of the weaknesses of these early circuit builders. He left school three days ahead of Graduation Day because he figured this would give him the jump on his schoolmates in finding a job. He landed one with the booking department of the vaudeville actors' protective organization known as The White Rats of America—"rats" being "star" spelled backwards. It did not pay much, but four dollars a week for a boy of twelve with a family of thirteen indigent Rubenses was helpful.

Two years later, he was already officially the manager and head mechanic of a penny arcade in an amusement park in Chicago. Actually, all he had to do was to yell, "All machines operate for pennies," and learn how to change a dime into nine or possibly eight cents.

The penny arcade life was too tranquil for Rubens, however, so he joined Harry LaThomas' Great Carnival Show. This impressive-sounding outfit consisted chiefly of a half-fed monkey looping the loop in a small automobile to which he was securely fastened. Everything was satisfactory until Mr. LaThomas insisted that Rubens ballyhoo in front of the show in a blond wig. Ambitious as he was, this, Jay felt, was asking too much, and he quit.

His next job was selling tickets, sweeping floors and posting bills for a dime museum. From there he graduated into business for himself. He opened up a chain of quick portrait postal card studios, known as "wet paper joints," because the cards were delivered wet to patrons. He also operated concessions in summer parks until he had accu-

When asked to ballyhoo the monkey act in a blond wig, Jules
quit and opened up a chain of wet paper joints.

mulated enough money to fulfill the ambition of his life, to own a picture theatre.

He found a closed one in Aurora, Illinois, which he bought, opened and painted red. Subsequent years and success did little to change him as a decorator. His scheme remained simple. "Make it any color you like as long as it's red."

For a while it looked as if his color had been a portentous choice for his Aurora theatre. His was one of three theatres in a comparatively small town and with two alert, experienced competitors, his receipts were woefully slim. The film companies, always eager to take advantage of a competitive situation, had the three owners bidding their heads off for pictures whose prices rose with every bid. Rubens cured the situation by buying out one of his competitors and by going into the garage business with the other. After a few sessions with the persuasive Rubens, the new partner readily saw the logic of Rubens' reasoning: Aurora had too many theatres; Aurora had too few garages; if he converted his theatre into a garage he would become the richest man in Aurora. In this fashion, Rubens achieved what is called a "closed situation" and with revenues channeled into one box office he proceeded to make back all the money he had lost, by underpaying the picture salesmen in direct ratio to the prices they had overcharged him. The directness of Rubens' ratio was roughly—against the salesmen—about four to one.

By the time I joined him in 1926 he had already obtained a similar stranglehold on about twelve other communities and was eying several more with ill-concealed interest. When Rubens wanted to move into a new situation, his emissary—frequently myself—would go into the town, check the "for rent" signs, the number of bars and poolrooms and the amount of business they were doing, and investigate the business of, and particularly the character of, the local movie house owner. I would return with a carefully documented report to which Rubens paid no attention whatsoever. Instead, he would descend in person for an interview with his prospective victim. He would make him some ridiculously low offer and follow it up with an eloquent discourse on the security and satisfaction the proprietor would enjoy once he exchanged the vicissitudes of conducting his own business for a weekly paycheck.

If repulsed, his next step was to get an option on some adjacent property, erect a huge sign depicting a palatial new theatre designed to make the Roxy look like the county poorhouse, and ostentatiously put a steam shovel to work. I would then be delegated to flood the local papers with stories that Great States had closed contracts cornering all the good pictures to be made in the next decade.

Our next, and usually final, move was into society. For this we always called in the invaluable services of Rubens' lawyer, Morris Leonard, not so much for his undeniable legal acumen as for his social graces. We attended fish-frys, dances and Wednesday night prayer meetings; we drank, shot pool, and became pals with the local politicians and newspapermen, and we promised the exhibitor's wife, the minister's sister and the banker's daughter that we would put them in the movies if they knew how to influence their menfolk for their own good. Morris was so popular that he was once a best man at the wedding of one of these pals, and on another occasion, and for another pal, served as a pallbearer. He looked appropriately miserable on both occasions.

These sacrifices on our part to the welfare of Great States almost invariably produced results. A deal would be worked out either to acquire the desired theatre for a fraction of its real worth or preferably on a partnership basis without any investment at all. Rubens recognized, long before the big circuit heads, the advisability of local partners who could retain the good will of the community and at the same time keep a close eye on the honesty and working habits of the hired staff. Once entrenched in a town, he would make "pooling" arrangements with any competitor who remained so as to obtain another closed situation. These pooling deals would vary all the way from "booking combines," in which Rubens purchased all the product for all the theatres in the town and divided it up with his competitors, to mergers in which all the receipts and sometimes all the expenses of the theatres involved would be shared on some basis that Rubens persuaded his rivals was a fair one. Once he made such a deal he kept it religiously. His record of reliability was as phenomenal as his acquisitive instinct.

In towns where his services were appreciated, Rubens would become one of the most loyal taxpayers and Chamber of Commerce boosters. And nothing aroused his protective instinct toward his adopted community as much as the threat of a visit by a carnival. Himself a graduate of out-of-door traveling shows, he knew and loathed all their tricks, which were indeed in those days raw. The famous old 1, 2, 3, swindle was perhaps the rawest. It is well described in Abel Green and Joe Laurie, Jr.'s *Show Biz* as the "Number Three" racket as follows: "This consisted of luring a likely male prospect into three tents—Tent No. 1, where he met a very amiable young woman; Tent No. 2, where he was sold a supply of rotgut for an anticipated lively evening; and Tent No. 3, where his pants pockets were picked without his knowledge (because he wasn't in them). Tent No. 3 was also sometimes used as the scene of the old badger game."

Rubens felt about out-of-door traveling shows the way Carrie Nation felt about saloons and he took care of them with the same crusading zeal. Aided by the Chamber of Commerce and the police department, few carnivals or gypsy outfits got past the unloading stage in any of his personally protected vicinities.

There were occasional towns where neighboring exhibitors refused to be neighborly. With such miscreants he also had no patience. He would rearrange the booking schedule for his own theatre or theatres even if it meant a daily change of pictures, so as to play every film released. He would then demand and obtain from the distributors twelve months' "protection," which meant that if any surviving independent theatre wanted to play a repeat engagement or what we call a "second run" of a picture which Rubens had shown, it could not do so for at least a year. Strengthened by his affiliation with Balaban & Katz—whose purchasing powers were such that it made it ill advised for any producer to sell pictures where they did not want them sold—Rubens was in a strategic position to demand favors, however unreasonable. Such practices today would promptly and properly land a man in Joliet penitentiary. In those days they only enabled Rubens to obtain complete control over Joliet as well as every other important Illinois community. They aroused no social disapprobation in a society conditioned to the exploits of railroad, oil and steel pioneers. Only his unfortunate competitors complained, and of these few survived. In his controlled towns Rubens was like the dying dictator who, when exhorted by his confessor to forgive his enemies, answered, "I have none. I have killed them all."

For business purposes rather than for personal taste, he maintained in those prohibition days a well-stocked suite in the strategically located Congress Hotel. There we lavishly entertained any New York and Hollywood executives who could be prevailed upon to stop over in Chicago, and whose unquenchable yen for high picture rentals could be assuaged by alcohol, feminine entertainment or a choice package of both.

One eminent sales manager got lost for a week en route from Los Angeles to New York. It cost Rubens plenty of his best Hennessey Three Star but it paid off the next time we made a contract for the distribution company's four-star pictures.

Such methods, I hasten to add, are no longer effective. Just as scientists have developed new strains of wheat or corn that are drought-resistant, the film companies have, over the years, bred a new species of sales chiefs impervious to the blandishments of liquor or ladies.

The Congress premises, however, were occasionally used

for purely social (or family) purposes. One case lingers nostalgically in my guilty memories. An adorable little blonde, newly married to an up-and-coming studio executive, passed through town. She was eager to see the sights and I was eager to show them. She had an incredible capacity for Scotch and I was no teetotaler. I awoke the next morning completely oblivious of what might have happened the night before but thoroughly well aware of who was sleeping in the twin bed next to mine. I dressed rapidly in a mood of deep repentance, returning later in the day laden with flowers and self-reproaches. I found the lovely lady equally remorseful. Her memory had also failed her but she insisted that whatever had occurred (if it had) was entirely her fault. Naturally, I insisted the fault was all mine. I sought to console her and she sought to cheer me. I wiped a tear from her eye, and she gave me a sisterly kiss of understanding. Sometime later I escorted her to her train.

Years later, when I was in a highly competitive situation and in dire need of pictures and my friend's husband had become a major company executive, he invariably came to my rescue. On one occasion, when his organization had encouraged me to believe it would rent my theatre a particularly desirable feature, which subsequently was sold to a larger house for a much greater rental than I could pay, I was given a substantial sum in settlement although there was no legal obligation to do so. Such generosity may be the customary procedure in other walks of life, but in the picture business it is so unprecedented as to suggest that I still had a friend at court. I mention the episode only as confirmation of my thesis of the superiority of luck over merit.

To my constant vexation, one of Jay's favorite pastimes was to change the policy of our theatres regardless of how successful they might be. He insisted on our booking bands into houses which were already doing capacity business; he wanted to play "flesh" every week-end although its popularity was rapidly waning and well-known performers were almost unobtainable. He had a yen for the legitimate theatre and never missed an opportunity to route into any of our theatres with stages any available road show, no matter how seedy it might be, and how completely it disrupted our customary policy.

The advent of sound, naturally, delighted his experimental showman's soul. The first Vitaphone shorts—one- or two-reel song, dance or comedy numbers—appeared in the summer of 1926. They left both the critics and the exhibitors in some uncertainty as to whether they were only a novelty or a profound revolution in movie technique. The cost of installing equipment in those early days was from twenty to thirty thousand dollars, but Rubens did not hesitate. One of my first assignments when I joined his organization was to see that every one of his better theatres was prepared to show sound pictures and, where regular equipment could not be obtained, to experiment with bootleg. These "just as good as Western Electric" sound devices were horrible, but Rubens didn't care as long as they made noise and as long as he was ahead of his competitors. When the first all-sound feature film, *Lights of New York*, was released, Great States was in a position to make a killing.

If Rubens were alive today, I am confident he would be installing television equipment in every theatre he controlled regardless of its current inadequacies, mechanical and entertainmentwise.

The wages of sin are frequently high profits. Undisturbed by any pangs of conscience, indeed regarding himself blandly as a benefactor of humanity engaged in bringing the best entertainment in the world to small communities and protecting them from the greedy or the depraved—*i.e.*, carnivals—Rubens rapidly created a small but highly efficient and prosperous circuit. He treated his henchmen generously and my own relations with him were highly agreeable. Prior to my coming he had heard unfavorable reports that I was a man of high principles, even honor, and had viewed my arrival with a jaundiced eye, but within a few months he was complaining to Sam Katz that I was being underpaid. Whether this was because he found me more or less honorable than he had anticipated I never ascertained. Nor did I get the raise.

One day in 1929 Sam Katz wrote a letter to Rubens asking his opinion about the future of vaudeville, which was then engaged in a struggle for existence with motion pictures. Rubens rarely answered letters. He was under the impression that no attention should be paid to communications the first time they were received. If they were of sufficient consequence or validity to merit attention, a second or third would, he was sure, be forthcoming. He had an appealing habit of tearing up bills and throwing the pieces out of the window. Only when he was displeased was a prompt reply forthcoming. I recall an offensive telegram which he received, and which he instantly answered, "Did not receive your wire."

When Katz's letter arrived, Rubens was out of town trying to promote a 50 per cent interest gratis in a theatre in Decatur. In his absence I dictated a detailed analysis of the situation. The years have since demonstrated substantial flaws in my reasoning. In fact, my prophecies were completely incorrect. At that time, however, they appeared plausible. What is more important, they fully coincided with Katz's opinions and he wired instructions that I join him immediately in New York.

· VII ·

PARAMOUNT-PUBLIX THEATRES was the largest theatre circuit ever organized. It was originally a wholly owned subsidiary of Adolph Zukor's Paramount-Famous-Lasky Company and grew with such rapidity that the parent company was soon reorganized under the name Paramount-Publix. At its height it boasted about eighteen hundred theatres in this country and additional ones in London, France, Belgium, Austria, Spain, Sweden, Mexico, Brazil; in Japan alone there were six.

It was composed of the big circuits which had emerged victors in their own territories, and of smaller circuits and theatres which had survived local onslaughts but whose owners finally came to believe, or were led to believe, that official membership in the Publix family was the way to glory or, at least, the way to eat. Great States, Rubin &

Finkelstein, Steve Lynch's Southern Enterprises, the Saenger Amusement Co., Nate Gordon's New England theatres and many other powerful organizations which I have not mentioned, all eventually wound up under the Publix banner. As did Balaban & Katz. And with it went Sam Katz —as president and general manager of all the Publix theatres.

When I joined Katz, a frenzied battle for theatres was being waged in every state in the Union. The chief contenders were Publix, Warner Brothers and the William Fox Company, with Loew's, now operated by the canny and cautious Nicholas Schenck, participating to a considerably lesser degree. A free-for-all of this nature was made to order for a man of Katz's ambition and temperament. Never inhibited by traditions of the past, he discarded old-fashioned methods involving threats and violence as too slow and archaic for the type of expansion he had in mind. His main objective was to acquire theatres with a minimum of bargaining and red tape. His ammunition was money—big money. He was prepared to outbid all offers made by competitors no matter how fantastic or how out of line with current earning values. This challenge was accepted by his equally aggressive competitors and the fracas that ensued was worthy of the highest standards of a fight-loving, expense-be-damned industry. I mentioned earlier that Publix had about eighteen hundred theatres at its height. My guess is as good as anybody's because nobody, with the possible exception of Katz, ever really knew. Zukor himself once said to an assistant, "About how many houses do you figure Sam has this morning?"

"About how many houses do you figure Sam has this morning?"

My office was in New York but I was assigned supervision of a vast territory stretching from Youngstown, Ohio,
to Grand Island, Nebraska. From there we proceeded to
move westward. In the process we acquired a seven-hun-
dred-seat theatre in North Platte, a prairie town with a
population of twelve thousand souls which also had a
smaller independent theatre. William Fox, powerfully entrenched in the Rocky Mountain area, regarded this as the
first step in an invasion of his God-given territory, and in
retaliation ordered the construction of a palatial new theatre which could well have graced Broadway or State
Street. On hearing of this, Mr. Zukor reacted as he would
to the rape of the Sabine women and declared that an
unprovoked assault had been made on one of his towns.
In order to teach Mr. Fox and all his other competitors
a lesson, he issued instructions that regardless of expense
we should build an even larger and more de luxe play-
house. We did. Before the competitive battle was over,
North Platte had three beautiful theatres, all losing money.

Two friends of mine in a Midwestern town saw no
reason why they should not share in the kind of bull
money that was being tossed around and decided to sell
their two theatres. They put a fast coat of paint on them
(the first in ten years), swept them out, installed new light
bulbs in the empty sockets, and invited inspection. A Publix
representative accepted their invitation with such alacrity
that within a week he was announced by their doorman as
being downstairs. In their office upstairs they pictured him
giving the place a detailed inspection. When they rushed
down to try to divert his attention from broken seats and

the lack of a cooling system, they found him sitting in his car with the chauffeur impatiently honking the horn. He briskly explained that he had no time to come in; he had the contract and the check in his pocket; he had decided on a price for the two houses which should be acceptable; he had no time to argue about minor matters; would they please sign here? Standing on the curb, they read the contract. They had made up their minds previously that they would demand thirty thousand dollars for the two houses and, if pressed, come down to twenty thousand dollars. The contract read forty thousand dollars for the two. My friends were no men to haggle about minor matters. They signed. He drove off.

Another owner I knew came in to the New York office to sell his profitable little theatre. I took him in to see Katz, who was, as usual, having a hectic day. "Don't bother me and take up my time with one house," he told my man. "Go out and get yourself a circuit and then come back." The owner walked down the street to the Warners, who were also too busy to bother with his single property.

Still another acquaintance sold his circuit at an unconscionable price to Fox merely because he had the foresight to arrange to be seen on frequent occasions playing golf with Katz's chief lieutenant, Sam Dembow.

Dembow is not only the best-dressed man in the industry but one highly unlikely to be swept off his feet by an incident however dramatic. He told me that the most memorable moments in the whole wild campaign for theatres occurred at the signing of the contract by which Paramount acquired the Comerford circuit in western Pennsylvania. This circuit, strategically located between Warner houses in eastern Pennsylvania and Warner houses in Ohio, seemed almost a necessity to Paramount to prevent Warners solidifying their grip on one of the most prosperous sections of the country. Dembow had long been pursuing old Mike Comerford and his son-in-law and chief aide, Frank Walker, later to become, under Roosevelt, Postmaster General of the United States. Publix's usual offer of payment in Paramount stock had little appeal to these hard-bitten businessmen. The only thing that talked, as far as they were concerned, was cash on the line.

At length a deal for fifteen million dollars was agreed upon. The papers were all prepared and all parties, including Dembow, gathered in Mr. Zukor's office for the final signing and the transfer of the check. As Mike Comerford took the pen in his hand he turned to Zukor, seated behind his desk and smoking a cigar as big as himself. "Adolph," he said, "before I sign this contract I ought to tell you that your company and mine are in a position at this moment each to make half a million dollars. Just before I came in here Warner offered me sixteen million dollars for my properties. Call this deal off and we'll split the overage between us."

Every eye turned to Zukor. He took a long, deep puff, paused for an instant that seemed like an hour, and said: "I have known you for twenty years, Mike, and I have never known you to welch on a deal. When you sign this contract for fifteen million dollars you will have enough money to enjoy every luxury that you, a simple man, could possibly desire. As for Paramount, I assure you that five hundred thousand means as little to us as the ashes on my cigar." And so saying, he flicked those ashes onto his super de luxe chenille carpet.

"If that's the way you feel," answered Comerford, "this is the way I act." And with a flourish he signed away a million dollars.

Others eager to cash in on the gold rush were not as honorable as Mike Comerford. I recall one occasion where every detail of a sale had been agreed upon and the papers prepared. At the last moment the lawyer for the seller made a belated and hangdog appearance. He said that his client, en route to our office, had been waylaid by a Fox representative who had offered him three hundred thousand dollars more than the three million dollars involved in our deal.

"But we have reached an agreement," protested Dembow. "He can't do this to us."

"I know he can't," answered the attorney, "but I am sorry to have to tell you that he has."

In addition to ready-made theatres, Publix constructed many houses of its own. Preceding these erections, if the proposed theatre was in my territory, I was delegated to check the traffic at various corners and observe where United Cigar or Liggett had located its stores, and how they were doing, because at that time we sought to locate theatres only in key locations. This practice eventually proved a grave error because of the ever-growing problems created by heavy traffic and parking. The most prosperous theatres today are not those located at the corner of Main and Market.

We were particularly partial to what we called "atmospheric theatres," the atmosphere supposedly having some connection with the historic background of the community. A theatre in Florida would be apt to have a bastard Spanish motif; in New Orleans it would be a rococo imitation of the French Renaissance, and when we didn't know what else to do, we constructed the "outdoor-indoor" theatre with thousands of false stars glittering in a false heaven.

The struggle for theatres raged until 1939—and a later story—but in the meantime, there was one project even closer to Katz's heart than rapid nation-wide expansion.

He was convinced that what has always been known as the show game could be converted into a legitimate businesslike enterprise. Never before or since has so sincere or elaborate an effort been made to effect this transformation. Working against all the mores and prejudices of movie men, he established a system of centralized management and supervision for Publix which compared favorably with the most progressive chain store operations and was modeled in efficiency and regimentation after a combination beehive and anthill.

To the average layman our procedures may not appear bizarre, but to the entertainment world, conditioned to intuition and the hunch system and peopled by a gypsy breed of nonconformists, it was a bloodcurdling phenomenon.

Local Publix theatre managers were supervised by district managers who in turn were supervised by division managers, all supervised by ten home office divisional directors, of whom I was, for a period, one.

In addition, the unfortunate managers were subjected to a steady stream of traveling experts in sound, projection, insurance, usher training, music, advertising, ventilation, not to mention long-nose auditors.

Every theatre had a budget broken down into eighty-eight items, no one of which could be increased even fractionally without the divisional director's written consent.

Based upon what similar theatres were doing in similar communities, there was also a receipt expectancy established, and woe betide the manager who fell too frequently below it.

Theatre schedules were conducted like railroad time-tables on a split-second basis. In Boston the last show had to go on at nine-twelve because the working hours in Boston required people to reach their offices at eight o'clock in the morning and they had to get home early. In more leisurely New York, the same show started thirty minutes later.

Indeed, the whole subject of "spills" was given careful scrutiny. Theatres doing a land-office business, as we were in our halcyon days, and as we assumed we would always continue to do, are dealers in time. By knowing how to move crowds in and out, a well-operated house can show better receipts in rush hours than a less efficiently managed one playing a more popular feature. We discovered that if early patrons, upon their arrival, were seated correctly, their exit could be facilitated so as to permit those waiting in the lobby to enter with less delay. Every usher had a little clocker in his hand with which he recorded the number of people going to the particular group of seats under his supervision. This information he relayed to the doorman and the doorman to the barker so that he could state, with some accuracy, how long the public would have to wait before admission.

There was a ventilation chart for every de luxe theatre, to record for the manager and later for his divisional director, the temperature at all times in his orchestra, balcony and lobby.

We published a pep magazine and we had conventions, drives, service buttons and prizes.

Manuals were prepared telling exactly what everyone in a theatre, from the manager to a janitor, should do in every conceivable emergency. We found out, by scientific tests, the number of janitors it took to clean a given floor area and the amount of cleaning material required for every kind of installation. We knew, for instance, what a certain cleaning material would do to calcimine and what it would not do for marble or brass. As for the manager, if a union delegate became obstreperous, or an outdoor circus came to town, or the cans containing the feature film failed to arrive, or a baby was born in a theatre aisle, or a set of teeth was left on a seat, all he had to do was to turn to the appropriate page and paragraph and learn how to handle the predicament.

An usher could never refer to an ancient with the term "elderly gentleman." Mindful of the sensitivities of age, the patron could only be called "gentleman" and addressed as "sir." Females of any age over puberty were always called "madam." For an attendant to snap his fingers to attract attention was cause for dishonorable discharge. If asked his opinion of a show, only one answer was permissible. "The comments are very favorable. I am sure you will enjoy it."

The purchase of all supplies was entrusted to trained buying agents located in the home office and all bills were audited and paid there. Everything was bought on a mass scale with many ensuing economies and the elimination of much petty graft, but also with a loss of the local good will which arose from the old-fashioned haphazard method by which the theatre manager patronized the merchants around the corner.

The manager had nothing to say about the pictures he played. They were bought for the entire circuit by bookers selected from all over the country for their ability to resist the blandishments of even the most persuasive distributors. The proper rental price for films has always been the chief bone of contention and an unfailing source of hostility between the producing-distributing companies and the theatre owners. Over the years many methods of film buying had been developed. One of these, for instance, was generally known, in honor of its creators, as the Rubin to Finkelstein play. In this routine, the two partners would engage in such an apparently bitter brawl that the salesman, fearful that he might be held responsible by his executives for provoking such hard feeling, took whatever deal was offered and hastily departed.

Another, the so-called Skouras treatment, was somewhat more subtle. One of the three brothers would take a recalcitrant position and refuse to make the slightest concession to the salesman's proposition. Another Skouras would fortuitously appear upon the scene, reprove his brother for treating the film companies unfairly, argue that he did not consider the salesman's position entirely unwarranted, and eventually work out a deal for him which the salesman was glad to accept although it was far less than what he had originally had in mind.

These time-consuming, cantankerous brawls had always offended Katz's yen for efficiency. At Publix, he sought more earnestly than anyone else has ever done in the movie business to contrive once and for all a reasonable and workable formula applicable to all pictures and fair to all concerned. Except for B's which he hoped would gradually disappear, he was prepared to pay film rentals on a basis of a graduating percentage of receipts rather than for a flat sum. A typical Publix deal for a picture, which eventually became quite prevalent throughout the industry, was 50 per cent of the theatre's receipts up to a point where the theatre's profit was 50 per cent of the producer's film rental, and after that a 50-50 split between them. Unfortunately, however, the more the producing-distributing companies received, the higher went their costs of production and the harsher deals they demanded. Over the years many things have changed in the industry but never the tendency for film rentals to rise.

In many cases, Publix, in its effort to satisfy the vendors and at the same time protect its theatre profits, worked out contracts so complicated that a knowledge of calculus and logarithms was required to figure the eventual film rental. The comments of the average unregenerate old theatre manager on these deals do not bear repetition. Half the fun of the whole business had been chiseling the distributors. If a picture could be purchased at a low flat price and played on a Sunday, he could make a killing, and it did not bother him unduly that if it were a bad picture it might drive patrons away for many months to come.

Publix film deals, however, were frequently arranged, over Katz's protests, in private conferences between the presidents of the various major companies and their sales chiefs. If Paramount product, for instance, was given a good break in all the Warner theatres, Mr. Zukor was usually prepared to promise that Warner pictures would be similarly well treated all over the Paramount-Publix circuit. In this fashion Publix usually wound up playing, in all situations where the circuits were not competitive, the pictures of Warner's, Loew's and Fox, the other leading producing-distributing-theatre-owning companies. This horse trading among the majors was grossly unfair to independent exhibitors (not to mention independent producers). Regardless of the merits of their theatres or the many years that they might have played the product of certain companies, they were ruthlessly, sometimes overnight, deprived of their product. In spite of their yells of anguish, however, it took twenty-nine years of continued litigation before an equity court eventually decreed that such practices were in restraint of trade.

Publix theatre managers had as little to say about advertising their pictures as they did about their purchase. A brochure was prepared in New York, again by the best specialists money could buy. For the first time in movie history newspaper advertising was analyzed and emphasis was laid on the elimination of superlatives and the use of focal spots as well as of more white space than had previously been customary. This was heresy to the old-fashioned manager. He loved black ads utilizing every inch of space with modest copy such as "150 of the world's most beautiful girls—150—in the greatest musical triumph of all time."

In addition to these brochures, wholesale help was sent out from the home office in the form of what we called *Jazz 'Em Up Catchlines*, applicable to any picture and suitable for all newspaper ads, posters and trailers. For instance:

Last-Time Lines: Today, tomorrow!—then gone! Just for two more hilarious [or heart-throbbing] days!

For Dramatic Pictures: Three years in the making! Maelstrom of emotions—every heart pang the screen can give is in it! See it for the greatest moments of your life. Your heart will race, your pulse will leap.

For Comedies: Here's the reel thing! A tailor-made roar—a maelstrom of glee and guffaws! The funny part of it is this—it's all funny from start to finish! You'll laugh louder, live longer! It's funny and fast and the laugh of your life!

Institutional: Fine programs carefully thought out—blending the best of screen and stage. Features and short subjects all combine to make the perfect entertainment. Another hit at headquarters. A Publix Theatre is your public's choice!

For our larger theatres we built stage shows along the lines of the Balaban & Katz presentations although even more lavish and, if possible, with less taste in scenery and costuming. The performers, regardless of cost, were obtained from the best Broadway talent available and we surrounded them with what, in our ignorance in those pre-Rockette days, we regarded as a well-trained line of girls.

The Balaban & Katz idea of stage shows, however, had been predicated on a prologue specially adapted to the feature film. The Publix shows were based on the theory of a balanced bill. For instance, for the film *Divorce*, the accompanying show was *Happy Days Are Here Again*.

Every Publix unit had a route all the way from Boston to Los Angeles and would travel the better part of a year. To produce the shows, Katz, as was his custom, sought the best known names obtainable. John Murray Anderson was lured away from the legitimate stage to become director of production. Boris Petroff was the ballet master. The music was in charge of Boris Morros, a fantastic character who purported, like all of his forefathers, to have been the leader of the Czar's Imperial Orchestra before the Bolsheviks chased him out of Russia. And, in and out of the picture, there was always Abe Balaban, the original presentation man.

In one year alone our stage shows employed over 1000 chorus girls, 46 ballroom dancers, 38 adagio dancers, 22 apache teams, 103 comedians, 92 acrobats, 51 blues singers, 25 operatic stars, 29 comedy songsters and 1018 musicians. To equip them properly we had more than 6000 costumes and 600 wigs.

Closely associated with Publix were the three fabulous Skouras brothers, whose rise from Greek bus boys in a restaurant to fame and fortune in the movie industry is a story which will, I trust, someday be told in all its incredible details to rekindle our faith in the American dream. The divisional directors of Publix were drawn from the ablest exhibitors in the country: men like Bob O'Donnell, now general manager of the Interstate circuit in Texas; John J. Fitzgibbons, now head of Famous Players Canadian Corporation; Marty Mullin, now chief of New England Theatres; and many more. Without exception they all had had far greater experience in show business than I. It was an honor to be associated with them and I learned much through their friendship and good-fellowship which would otherwise have taken me years to acquire.

Most of these men and their assistants were graduates of the circus, vaudeville, or legitimate theatres. In their own field there were few problems that their ingenious showmanship and disdain for hours of work could not overcome. Behind home office desks, however, buried in budgets, charts, letters, reports and forms to be signed in triplicate, they were miscast and miserable. Not only did we have to read letters incessantly, we had to write lengthy monthly reports and even lengthier semiannual ones. It was my conviction that no one ever read these documents and I demonstrated it to my satisfaction by inserting in the middle of one of mine an estimate of the devastating effect upon the American forests that a long-sustained Publix paper operation would entail. It passed unnoticed.

Sensing their opposition and disliking their haphazard methods as much as they disapproved of his businesslike ones, Katz hoped eventually to replace the old-time theatre managers with well-trained college graduates. I once heard him say in a speech to Harvard students, "We never appeal to the material senses in merchandising what we have to sell. Our entire subject is a psychological one—it might almost be called a whimsical one at times. At any rate, it is a business appealing to the imagination. And that is why we want college graduates."

To train these graduates properly, we conducted a six-months course in every aspect of theatre operation. We started our graduates off at fifty dollars a week and this was raised in time up to one hundred dollars, but unfortunately, the old Publix school tie failed to inspire ardent loyalty in its wearers. Other circuit operators who did not care to spend money to maintain a school merely stood waiting on the street corners flashing money; they got our graduates almost as fast as we turned them out.

We lost some promising alumni in other fashions also. I remember that on one occasion I had the brilliant idea of instructing each new small-town manager in my division to call daily on not less than six families and to invite them, if they were not attending his theatre, to come there in the near future as his personal guests. In this fashion I figured that a conscientious manager could become friendly with close to two thousand families a year. I underestimated my men. They carried out my orders so assiduously that within one season one was elected mayor of his town, two were chosen to the Town Council and two became popular executives of the local Chamber of Commerce. In these positions they proved base ingrates and refused to grant Publix any special favors.

My territory for Publix included Waterloo, Iowa, where we operated three theatres. One of the most important employees of a small-town theatre in those days was the bill poster, who covered weekly many miles putting everything from 3-sheets to 24-sheets on barns, silos and even outhouses. One of the best of these bill posters was John Blum. He covered the countryside in a fiery red 1912 Ford, which could be seen for miles and heard even farther. He always traveled accompanied by his terrier, Tag, who had a capacity to sit on the radiator of the car regardless of speed or the condition of the roads. Tag could perform tricks from begging a farmer to let John post his paper, to looking appealingly at the farmer's wife and saying "mama" or a fair replica thereof. I promised John a substantial raise if Tag could ever learn to say "Paramount," but that was a bark beyond him.

Considerable time and analysis were put in on what was documented as "Theatre Manager Alibis." Broken down, this impressive-sounding study revealed, in summary, the following familiar laments:

Each winter there is the biggest blizzard since 1888.

September business is off because the parents are busy getting the kids ready for school and October business is worse because the kids are all in school.

In November, of course, there are the elections and the big football games.

In December everyone is too busy Christmas shopping to go to the theatre and in January they have spent all of their money on shopping so they can't afford to go to the theatre.

In April there is Lent. In May, daylight saving; and in June a young man's as well as a young woman's fancies turn to love-making outdoors rather than in the theatre balcony.

The summer, of course, is the hottest in history.

Appropriate steps were taken to try to remedy and bolster such inexcusable excuses.

On one occasion it was decreed that all ace Publix theatres, regardless of local tradition or expense, must be rechristened to bear the Paramount name. I was assigned to the conversion of the well-established Riviera of Omaha, Nebraska. Never one who, given a blank check, ever ducked a campaign, I plastered Omaha's billboards, busses and business windows for weeks with slogans celebrating the public's overwhelming demand for a new name for its favorite Publix theatre.

Came the day of the big christening and there arrived a quartet of Paramount's most illustrious brass, headed by Adolph Zukor himself. I hurried them to a waiting taxi.

"To the Paramount," I proudly instructed the driver.

"Where?" he asked.

"To the Paramount Theatre," I replied.

"Never heard of it."

I weakly explained, "To your right and up the hill."

"Oh," he brightened, "you must be meaning the Riviera."

"Did you say this campaign cost twenty thousand dollars?" asked Mr. Zukor.

· VIII ·

In spite of my admiration for Katz's talents and tenacity, I had many reservations about Publix's centralized management system. With the courage engendered by a long-term contract in my pocket, I expressed myself so boldly and so frequently that it was found advisable either to demote or promote me—I am still not sure which. Anyhow, I was divorced from Publix activities and made director of advertising, exploitation and publicity for the producing and distribution organization. My headquarters were New York. The West Coast offices, technically under my supervision, were manned by Frank Whitbeck and Arch Reeve. As a result of their wisdom and forbearance and of various subtle devices of my own, I survived in this job for close to two years. Had I held it for twenty I would never have acquired the skill or the national influence of men like Howard Dietz at M-G-M or Charlie Einfeld at Twentieth Century-Fox, or Max Youngstein at United Artists.

The greener you are, the greener the grass in the other fellow's pasture, and knowing nothing at all about their problems, it is my envious guess that a similar job with an outfit like, say, General Motors, must be a cinch. They put out one new model of each of their cars a year and are given adequate time and information to create thoughtful and thorough advertising campaigns for them. Paramount produced a picture a week (not to mention shorts and a newsreel), and expected a General Motors-caliber campaign for every one of them. Exploiters of cars and other such utilitarian wares, furthermore, do not have to submit lines or credits to producers, associate producers, directors, associate directors, salesmen, theatre operators, censors, authors, actors and actresses, their agents and all their in-laws.

It is possible, of course, that they, on the other hand, regard movies with an envious eye, thinking that our line of merchandise is glamour and that screen stars must be "awfully interesting people to meet" and publicizing them must be a continuous round of cocktail parties and pleasant dalliance.

Association with performers has not altogether disenchanted me—I have admired many, thought myself enamored of several and have even liked a few—but it seems to me I have met more glamorous, not to mention better, performers among Chevrolets. And no Chevrolet would ever climb up a ladder high above the street to measure the size of his (or her) name, and then call me at three o'clock in the morning to complain that it was one-sixteenth of an inch smaller than the contract specified—or less impressive than a fellow artist's. For some unascertainable reason, Hollywood personalities could never convey their complaints at any hour earlier than three A.M. New York time, and for two years I was awakened on the average of three or four nights a week to be rebuked or cajoled by actors, producers, directors and authors. One actor-author who could be counted on not to complain about split credits or size or secondary billing of his name was the one who appeared in the ad: "Mary Pickford and Douglas Fairbanks co-starred in their first talking picture, *The Taming of the Shrew*, by William Shakespeare, with additional dialogue by Sam Taylor."

Charlie Washburn, the noted Broadway press agent, worked as a carnival publicist in his early days and one night when the barker for The Great Fearlesso failed to show up, Charlie substituted for him. The Great Fearlesso was a daredevil motorcycle rider, who, until the night Charlie took over, had always lived up to his billing. Charlie filled his new assignment with such ringing phrases as "Should this man live," "Death-defying," "Few have survived," "Hair-raising terror at every turn," and "Death rides with him tonight." Listening to Charlie's pitch, Fearlesso got so scared he refused to go on.

That is what is known as falling over your own feedbag. We never reached such heights at Paramount—a performer who is so influenced as to refuse to perform is the tops in testimonial tribute—but it is a universal trait in the major-

116

ity of actors (as with military brass, big business executives, politicians, revivalists and other performers) to believe what is written about them—at least, if it is favorable. We had our share of the susceptible.

On one occasion we were instructed to assign to one actress—whose raw material hardly warranted it—the role of "deadly siren." Until the campaign was under way she had been unaware that she had such qualities, but after reading all the synthetic stories and publicity blurbs which we indefatigably planted in newspapers, weeklies and on the radio, our creation not only lived up to the part but was soon bawling the blazes out of us for a photo in the Burlington *Hawkeye Gazette* which captioned her modestly as "feminine pulchritude personified." "Tough" actors who couldn't fight their way out of a Dixie cup often overestimated our publicity and their strength and we would then have the additional assignment of keeping their lost battles and black eyes out of print and their persons out of the hoosegow. After reading scintillating copy under their own by-lines, which came out of our joke files, "noted wits" often became highly critical of us when our copy failed to live up to their own editorial standards. And an actor who has read a few best sellers (or bought an original painting) and who is publicized as "cultured" can nearly always be counted upon to become socially unbearable.

Harry Reichenbach, the greatest of all movie publicists, in writing on this common beef—the ingratitude of actors to us creators—used to tell about his dealings with Rudolph Valentino. It was, he said, through his efforts that Valentino got his first opportunity to act with Clara Kimball

Young in *The Eyes of Youth*. Without further help from Reichenbach he reached stardom and they did not again meet until Harry was called in by Valentino's producer to handle his publicity.

Harry visited Valentino in his dressing room and a valet answered his knock and asked what he wanted.

"Tell him Harry Reichenbach wants to see him."

"Does Mr. Valentino know you?"

"I think so," said Harry. "He used to borrow a buck at a time from me and he always knew who to bring them back to."

The valet withdrew into the dressing room and soon returned with the brush-off, "Mr. Valentino is resting just now. He is very tired. He suggests that you see Mrs. Valentino as she handles all his publicity matters."

Mrs. Valentino was seen and, after looking at the material Harry had prepared, vetoed everything. Harry, in turn, vetoed the Valentinos and stalked off the lot.

Later on, however, when Valentino's popularity was slipping (he had to die to revive it), another rescue call was sent to Reichenbach, who, with his usual ingenuity, suggested that the star grow a beard. Which he did. This was calculated to excite the Master Barbers Association of America, and under some subtle prodding from Reichenbach, they passed a resolution that unless Valentino forthwith had his beard removed, they would boycott his pictures. Eventually, after much publicized bartering with the barbers, Valentino consented to have it shaved off in the presence of a large and deeply impressed audience.

The remains of the controversial beard are now in a Western museum.

My troubles were not confined to Hollywood talent. The head of our sales department chronically complained that my copy was not sufficiently "trite." Exhibitors groused that the advertising was too refined, while Mr. Hays' Motion Picture Association of America found it too salacious. Mr. Hays himself once said, "The trouble with you, Mr. Mayer, is you don't know the difference between decency and indecency." My boss, Adolph Zukor, concurred. For Mae West's first starring role I selected a luscious portrait of her which embellished at strategic points what nature had already so bountifully blessed. Underneath it I wrote a few words of chaste advertising copy, phrased artfully (in my opinion) to avoid controversy or rebuke. It read, "Hitting the high spots of lusty entertainment." This I submitted to Mr. Zukor, who refrained from comment until the advertising material had been prepared and distributed and could no longer be recalled. Then he summoned me into his presence and spoke to me sadly, as to an erring son.

"Mr. Mayer," he said, "I thought you were such a lovely gentleman, and yet, in times like these [it was in 1932 and grosses were heartbreaking] you use a dirty word."

I tried to explain that nothing could be further from the truth; that the word was not dirty, and that I was indeed a lovely gentleman, distinguished for my purity and refinement.

"Lusty," he answered. "Lusty! What a word to use at such a time!"

I tried next to overwhelm him with my high-flown knowledge and to explain that lusty was a close relative of the German word *"lustig,"* implying vigorous and full of life.

"No need to tell me what lusty means," he countered. "When I look at those beautiful busts I know what lusty means."

Mae was one of the few stars with whom my contacts were, so to speak, occasionally in the flesh rather than through the extensive card indexes in my office. It was chiefly through these files that I became acquainted with (and publicized) the boyish modesty of Gary Cooper, Cary Grant's irresistible dimple, Chevalier's Gallic charm, Chester Morris' tricks as a magician; and while I never met Jeanette MacDonald I knew her exact bust and hip measurements, the color of her eyes and hair and her operatic ambitions. I also knew—from Hollywood runners—that owing to her somewhat heavy-handedness as an actress she was privately referred to as "the cast-iron canary." Through my files I also became personally acquainted with Kay Francis' lisp, Herbert Marshall's wooden leg and Clive Brook's toupee (size 8½), the gangster past of one of our rising young men and the capacity for booze of one of our declining young women ("highly unreliable for personal appearances," my records warned me).

The first time I saw Mae West was during the filming of *Night After Night,* her first picture and one in which she had only a minor role. In it a hat check girl took one look at Mae's tiara and, almost collapsing on the counter, exclaimed. "Goodness, what beautiful diamonds!" Mae

"No need to tell me what lusty means."

answered with a line improvised on the spot by herself and delivered with that perfection of timing which was her supreme asset, "Goodness had nothing to do with it, dearie."

As is the case with many stars, Mae was the recipient of much erotic fan mail. Most stars who evoke this kind of adulation—George Raft was one who inspired particular frankness in his lady fans—are somewhat shamefaced about it. Not Mae. She kept all her letters, pictures and propositions in a bulging file and framed some of the most virile. The only time she ever suggested that I come up and see her, in fact, was to see and read these testimonials.

When Mae was first signed up, I was notified that another distinguished female personality had also put her signature on a Paramount contract. That Mae would make the grade was considered highly dubious, but concerning the success of the other it was conceded that there could be no question. She was the world-famous radio star, Kate Smith. Our production geniuses promptly proceeded to build for Kate a simple two-million-dollar musical appropriately entitled *Hello Everybody*. It was so dull and top-heavy that in spite of her golden voice it proved a complete failure and in a short time she was given, and was back on the air. Mae, on the other hand, zoomed overnight to a national phenomenon. In both 1933 and 1934 she was voted by the exhibitors as their best money-making star. In 1933 she was being paid two hundred thousand a picture.

By 1936 she found it difficult to get a contract. The rise and fall of the West was rapid, but while it lasted sex was ripsnorting. It was at the height of my "sex" campaign for her that a special meeting was held at the Hays Office of all the advertising heads of the picture companies. These meetings were usually called when there was sufficient evidence that our campaigns had, in Hays' estimation, gone too far. On this occasion he found grave fault with us. Our illustrations were more horizontal than vertical, our ladies' low necklines were approaching their high skirtlines, there were too many ads of torrid clinches, and the copy of one campaign in particular, he said meaningfully, was full of such innuendoes and vice that it was making a mockery of the sacredness of the sexes. As the eloquent ex-Postmaster General of the United States continued to read further indictments, a pair of those perennially amorous New York pigeons lit on the ledge of the window outside. All eyes turned toward them and followed their uninhibited proceedings. Hays sensed a diversion of interest and, looking up from his notes and over his spectacles, saw the turned heads. "What's going on out there?" he asked. Si Seadler, M-G-M's irrepressible advertising manager, lowered his eyelids shyly, pointed to the window and said, "They're violating the Production Code, sir."

Other Paramount stars whom I met outside of my card indexes were Jack Oakie, who frequently found fault with both my ads and my ready-made clothes. Both lacked class and color. "You'll never be a success in this business," he told me, "until you get yourself a decent tailor. You look like a duffel bag." Claudette Colbert was a co-operative darling as was Carole Lombard. And Miriam Hopkins needed no ghost writer to make her entertaining. Nor, needless to say, did Robert Benchley. I called on Benchley once in Hollywood at his bungalow at the sun-drenched Garden of Allah and found him in his shorts sitting inside under a sun lamp. I pointed out that with a few steps he could be out of doors and under nature's sun. "I don't trust nature," he shuddered. "Out there things can fall on you. Like meteors. Or manna."

Benchley was not a man given to practical jokes, but, once in Hollywood, he was the author of one which is still talked about. Among the varied and assorted people who were his friends there was a doctor who although called a quack by the critical was to the sympathetic Benchley merely experimental. And earnest. In his experiments with the common cold, hangovers, headaches, flea-bites and such, Benchley was his willing guinea pig. He swallowed pills for him and allowed himself to be studied for results. The doctor branched out once, however. He invented a pill which he believed would cure lost manhood, and wanted to try it out. His guinea pig felt this was going too far. He took the pills but when the doctor called on him the next day for the checkup, Benchley was ready for him.

No, he reported, there had been no change in temperature. No, he had remained exceedingly calm. No, he had felt no warmth or flutter. He had been excited only by a Rex Stout murder story he had read all night. Yes, he had taken the full dose. The doctor scratched his head and protested that there must have been some kind of change somewhere, somehow.

"Nothing at all," said Benchley, "except maybe this." He dropped his pajama pants and showed him the base of his spine. On it, with the painstaking help of his friend Roland Young, he had glued a small but graphic sprouting of rooster tail feathers.

I also remember Silvia Sidney. Sylvia had her heart set on playing the part, in Cecil B. DeMille's *Sign of the Cross*, of a vestal virgin of high Roman pedigree who embraced Christianity and died a martyr to her new-found faith. Sylvia is a fine actress fully qualified to play many major roles. She is, however, a Brooklyn girl with a lusty, busty form of Semitic beauty and physically scarcely built for the role. She was, however, a protégée of Mr. Schulberg's, and he was at that time the dynamic head of the Paramount studio. A battle of titanic proportions broke out and only through the intervention of the anti-Schulberg forces was the part finally wrenched away and given to the more appropriately proportioned, if less toothsome, Elissa Landi. In passing, it might be remarked that no studio head with whom I have ever worked was more co-operative or sympathetic than Schulberg.

The most glamorous of all our stars was Mary Magdalene von Losch. Born in Berlin in 1904, she is the only living actress who would confess to so prehistoric an origin and, my wife excepted, she is the most seductive grandmother in all history. She is today known as Marlene Dietrich.

Her first role was in a German version of *Broadway*. When Josef von Sternberg (the "von" is strictly a phony) went to Germany to produce Emil Jannings' first talkie for UFA, he arrived at a dance hall where Marlene was appearing, just in time to hear her speak one near-English line: "Three chjeers for the jentleman who has just von grand prize." Joe was so entranced by her enunciation, the brooding melancholy of her face which he interpreted as indicating suppressed passion, and her long, beautiful legs that he immediately engaged her to play opposite Emil Jannings in *Blue Angel*.

The public shared von Sternberg's appreciation of her charms. In spite of Jannings' hamming as a lovesick professor (it was the picture in which he eventually strangled Marlene, you may remember, while yelling at the top of his lungs, "cock-a-doodle-doo"), Dietrich scored a sensational personal triumph. Joe promptly signed her to a long-term contract and brought her back to Hollywood with him. She arrived in New York with only twelve pieces of luggage, including a saw which she played with a bow. Never since has she crossed the Atlantic so miserably equipped.

Her first American picture was *Morocco*, in which von Sternberg transformed her from a *saftig*, unsophisticated German *Maedchen* into a svelte and sultry enchantress. Marlene was Trilby to Joe's Svengali. She did all her studying and rehearsing in front of him. He did not wish her to have any conception of her own, only his, as to how to read lines or perform her part. Also I suspect that he insisted on her retaining her German accent as another indication of her exotic quality. Certainly she spoke better English in *Morocco* than she was speaking a few years later in other pictures. And far better than the only time I was ever alone with her—a beautiful moonlit evening—when suddenly she could neither speak nor understand a word of English.

Morocco, however, was followed by a series of deplorable films in which, staggering under jewels and aigrettes, all the acting Marlene could do was to lie languorously on a chaise longue exposing as much of her lovely limbs as the Hays Office would sanction. Under Joe, she made five more pictures in four years—*Dishonored, Shanghai Express, Blonde Venus, Scarlet Empress, The Devil Is a Woman.*

In 1932 Mrs. Reza von Sternberg sued Marlene for five hundred thousand dollars for alienation of her husband's affections and one hundred thousand dollars for libel. No sooner had our legal department got this matter out of the courts—and, more important, out of the headlines—than von Sternberg had a quarrel with Schulberg over the script of *Blonde Venus,* of which Joe was the proud and sensitive author. Von Sternberg walked off the set, followed by Miss Dietrich.

Almost simultaneously, we received half a dozen wires from Hollywood frantically describing how Marlene had taken to wearing pants. At this time slacks were still a novelty in the United States and their use was deemed almost as shocking to the female public as the wearing of bloomers had been fifty years previously. The male public felt that trousers should be reserved for men as a vestigial remnant of their former supremacy. We pleaded with Marlene to give them up but she was adamant.

We finally had no recourse except to seek to make an asset out of our dilemma. We turned our attention from films to feminine attire and spent more time with the elegantly tailored lady editors of *Vogue* and with Kelcey Allen of *Women's Wear* than with the cheesecake editors of other journals. Fortunately for us, business in cloaks and suits was bad and the manufacturers welcomed the appearance of a new garment for women. We rode on the crest of a wave of slacks which swept the entire country. Large rears, exposed from Maine to Oregon, should have rested heavily upon our consciences. But they didn't. We had made Marlene's trousered legs more fabulous than ever.

When Marlene sailed for Europe in 1933 she was wearing pants, a black Homburg and a man's overcoat. She said she would continue to wear masculine clothes, but counseled other women against them. Needless to say, they did not heed her.

Wilson Mizner, the famous wit, bitterly attributed the whole backward trend to us. He wrote to a friend, "They are now even wearing coats and vests, the short ones looking like pinchbottles while the size 46's remind me of the tonneaus of the old Panhards that you had to crank."

I was fortunate during those years in having many wonderful films to publicize. The Marx Brothers were at their zany best—and what a best it was—in *Horse Feathers* and *Monkey Business*. Maurice Chevalier was directed by Rouben Mamoulian in *Love Me Tonight* and by Ernst Lubitsch in *One Hour with You*. The superbly skillful Mamoulian also directed *Dr. Jekyll and Mr. Hyde* with Fredric March and Miriam Hopkins. One of the prize-winning pictures of 1932 was Frank Borzage's *A Farewell to Arms* with Helen Hayes, Gary Cooper and Adolphe Menjou. One of the best comedies made in that year or any other was *Million Dollar Legs* with W. C. Fields and Jack Oakie. It was unsuccessful. As was *If I Had a Million,* an unforgettable series of episodes acted and directed by all the top-ranking personalities on the Paramount lot.

Good films or bad, we had to exploit them one and all by every possible means. *The Phantom President* was taken to Washington, where it was seen by F. D. R. George M. Cohan was the star of the picture but he disliked it intensely and said so publicly, which was a great help. For *The Devil Is Driving* we hired half a dozen daredevil drivers to speed their racing cars across the continent. One of them was badly injured, which, however regrettable, also proved useful. *Sky Bride* was exploited by the wedding of two young people at an altitude of ten thousand feet. On one occasion we imported a hippopotamus for a jungle scene. Unfortunately no one had ever told us that hippos can't swim in salt water. We put him in the Pacific. He never reappeared even for a bow.

Possibly our most noteworthy campaign was in connection with the film version of H. G. Wells' mystery thriller, *The Island of Dr. Moreau*, rechristened for movie purposes *The Island of Lost Souls*, and starring Charles Laughton, who was still comparatively unknown in this country. It appeared obvious that the picture, even bolstered by the pleasing presence of Bela Lugosi, would require a substantial injection of publicity adrenalin if it were to accumulate healthy grosses. In an inspired moment we decided to promote a nation-wide contest to discover a young woman to play the leading feminine role of a lovely girl slated to be transformed into a beast. The victor was to be crowned "The Panther Woman of America."

To our amazement, the announcement created a sen-

129

sation. All over the country, attractive lassies, regardless of rosy cheeks and dovelike features, flooded the offices of the newspapers with whom we were co-operating, to make their bid for this feline short cut to fame and fortune. Local winners, the Panther Woman of Dixie, New England, Rocky Mountains and the like, were transported to Hollywood for the final eliminations. Strangely enough, those who came accompanied by mothers did not last as long as the unchaperoned ones. Among these, the final victor was a charming though scarcely talented young woman from Chicago, where, by a peculiar coincidence, Paramount happened to operate more theatres than in any other city.

In addition to a complete lack of picture experience, the Champ had one other liability. She resembled a panther as much as Boris Karloff looks like a lamb. To offset this defect we confided to the public that her loyalty to the puma family, which had elevated her to stardom, was so intense that she had adopted a baby panther as her inseparable companion and had sworn never to let it out of her arms, so fierce was her mother love for it. Unfortunately, I made this announcement without research. Subsequently, we searched the menageries and circuses to no avail. No baby panther could be located. Eventually, we compromised on a baby leopard and, movie fans apparently not being avid students of animal life, nobody was one whit the wiser.

All went well for a few months until the leopard started to grow up and take nibbles from tempting portions of the lady's anatomy. Halfway through the picture she announced that either the leopard or the Panther Woman was quitting. Although we had columns of publicity in practically every newspaper in the country, it should be added that the picture proved a resounding dud. No promotion campaign, regardless of its fanfare and its acceptance by the fans, is a substitute for old-fashioned word-of-mouth audience approval.

Another earlier leopard who left her spots, according to Jesse Lasky, on movie history was "Minnie," who starred with Thomas Meighan and Gloria Swanson in *Male and Female*. The script called for Meighan, as the admirable butler, to shoot Minnie with a homemade bow and arrow just as she was about to leap on Gloria and tear her lovely limb from limb. Tom was then to throw the animal's carcass over his shoulder and saunter back to camp, loitering only long enough for some affectionate dalliance with the grateful Gloria.

In the early sequences, skillful cutting made it appear that Minnie was on the loose, when actually she was confined behind powerful barbed wires, and it had been agreed that for the subsequent scenes a stuffed leopard should be dangled like a fur neckpiece around Meighan's shoulders. Cecil DeMille, the director, is, however, a perfectionist, and nothing could persuade him to accept a limp and floppy remnant of a once-magnificent wild beast supplied by the property man. On the other hand, nothing could persuade Meighan to tangle with a live leopard. The resourceful DeMille came up with a solution: Minnie had to be chloroformed. This was accomplished with big hunks of meat, plenty of sponges and bloodcurdling roars of rage.

The supine creature was then draped over the shoulder of the none too enthusiastic Meighan and the cameras began to grind for the love scene with Gloria, not to mention a delegation of guards armed with Winchesters out of camera range. DeMille, furthermore, is no man to hurry over a big heart throb. In the middle of the third take, Minnie began to show signs of returning consciousness.

"She's coming to," shouted Tom.

"Keep on just a moment more. Don't be afraid," yelled DeMille from a safe distance.

"I love you—I love you," murmured the magnificent Gloria—to whom, it was uncertain.

As the welcome word "cut" was spoken, the gallant stars established a new Hollywood record for sprinting exits.

Probably the most harrowing experience in my publicity career was in connection with the film *The Man I Killed*. A Houdini imitator, whose claim to fame consisted of the ability to be buried for twenty-four hours without suffering suffocation, volunteered his services for a day, for a month's salary. After much promoted controversy in the press as to the desirability of running so grave a risk, we buried our man alive one evening, carefully marking the spot where he was interred with a tracing of lime. The next evening, when we started to dig him up, we discovered that a storm which had hit the vicinity during the night had washed away all traces of lime. It took half the night and a crew of thirty diggers finally to locate him. He was none the worse for his experience. He was in much better shape, in fact, than I. With some propriety he demanded double overtime for his extra hours.

Not long after this episode, the home office had a brainstorm and overnight decreed that the title of *The Man I Killed* was to be changed to *Broken Melody*. The picture was already playing at the Criterion Theatre and the name had been publicized for many months and thousands of dollars of advertising accessories had been distributed. But the picture was doing badly and a culprit had to be found. In this case it was the title. I know of no instance where altering a title has proved effective once a picture has been released. Nonetheless, these later-than-last-minute changes are a common occurrence in the life of every advertising director.

As far back as 1913 James Barrie's *Half an Hour* was eventually changed to *The Doctor's Secret*, its producers fearing the public would dismiss it as a short. Only recently, as intelligent and farsighted a studio head as Dore Schary of M-G-M asked me what I thought of changing a poor title on a good picture—*Angels in the Outfield*—which was not doing anything approximating the business that its merits justified. Other recent examples are *U.S.S. Teakettle*, a highly amusing *New Yorker* story rechristened *You're in the Navy Now*. Paramount's unusual, if somewhat downbeat, *Ace in the Hole* was changed to *The Big Carnival*, *The Goldbergs* to *Molly* under the impression that anti-Semitism rather than dullness was the cause of its trouble, and *Queen for a Day* to *Horsey*, the idea being apparently that horses are more popular these days than royalty. None of these changes improved business enough to pay for the expenses they entailed.

I know a small-town exhibitor who changes titles whenever he sees fit and claims that he frequently has excellent results with pictures which do badly elsewhere. He altered *The Asphalt Jungle* to *Babes and Bullets* and *Ticket to Tomahawk* to *Sheriff's Daughter*. I think, however, he stretched things a bit too tight when he rechristened *Week-End of Love* to *Father Buys a Corset*.

When at a later date I went into the film-importing business, my partner and I argued for days about the title *Open City*. We did not change it for only one reason: we could not agree on a better one. It proved an unexpected box-office bonanza because patrons, instead of understanding that it meant a city immune to armed attack, thought it denoted a wide-open town where vice and depravity flourished. For over a year we had on our shelves a film version of Graham Greene's *Brighton Rock*. No exhibitor evinced the least interest in showing the picture until we had a wild idea one day and rechristened it *Young Scarface*. It was immediately in demand but Howard Hughes, who had produced *Scarface*, threatened to sue me unless we found another title.

Harold Lloyd's *Mad Wednesday* was conceived as *An Innocent Affair*. Then it became *Don't Trust Your Husband*. Finally it was released as *The Sin of Harold Diddlebock*, and when unsuccessful, guess how it ended up: *Mad Wednesday*.

Possibly the last word on title changes was a notice written by the well-known ribster, Bob Condon, and posted on the Eagle Lion bulletin board:

"The picture, *The Noose Hangs High*, will be retitled *Laughter on the Gallows*.

"*The Noose Hangs High* was formerly titled *The Tight Necktie* and was adapted from the novel, *Give Him Some Rope.*

"In all communications please refer to the picture as *Laughter on the Gallows.* A rough print, unscored, now has the working title, *Laugh Till You Choke.* The finished print will carry the final title. If further changes come through you will be notified.

"*Laughter on the Gallows* was once a play which closed out of town with the title, *Hemp Jig.*

"Please change all stories on *The Noose Hangs High* to read *Laughter on the Gallows.* The title of the radio serial based on the play and the novel was *John's Other Wife.*" (*Variety,* 7/30/51.)

As head of the publicity department, I was given strict instructions constantly to emphasize Hollywood's high moral standards. We had figures to prove that it boasted the country's highest contribution per capita for charitable causes and the lowest per capita for crime. We claimed fewer divorces and more happily married couples with three children, a Ford and a dog than any other city of similar size in America. Personally, I am convinced that the persistent effort to make Hollywood appear a citadel of virtue and nobility has been a grave error. Even the endeavor to make picture personalities seem average or "just nice folks" has done much to dispel those very qualities of glamour and allure which once made Hollywood names and faces celebrated throughout the world. The pleasures of identification and vicarious adventure through the person of some well-known star have enlivened many a dull life—as well as made many a dull picture profitable.

The tendency of certain actors to use their fists too readily, and of certain actresses to bestow their affections too easily, has never injured their popularity at the box office of the big cities. When Robert Mitchum was arrested in a dope raid, far from arresting his career, it advanced it. Performers' fan mail rises with each divorce. Franchot Tone's indiscreet conduct did not add tone to the stature of the industry but I am certain that, given a suitable vehicle, millions of fans will flock to see him. As an Academy Award-winning writer said recently, "The sooner we go back to keeping pet cobras and driving snow-white Rolls Royces the better off we'll be."

Hollywood is vulnerable to assault from innumerable hostile quarters. In my days it was reviled by intellectuals as reactionary because it found more profit in making escapist than in "message" films. Today it is denounced as unpatriotic on the flimsy basis that a small percentage of its writers and actors fell for the Communist line. The habits of its celebrities, social, political or sexual, are actually only an excuse, not a cause, for the never-ending hatred of pressure groups, anti-Semites, bluenoses and demagogues of every kind. National susceptibilities are also a constant source of grief. When we made *A Farewell to Arms* at Paramount, we were forced to change the entire section which showed Italian troops in retreat. Apparently Italian armies, like American armies, never "retreat" but instead "make strategic withdrawals." When the villain of one of our pictures had a Mexican name, our pictures were banned in Mexico until he was rechristened. *Madam*

Butterfly was rejected by the Japanese censors because Sylvia Sidney threw her arms around her American hero's neck, baring her elbow in a fashion which appeared obscene to strait-laced Orientals. You are also apt to get into trouble at home when you try to adopt the idiom of a foreign land. In a picture supposedly located in Japan, Gary Cooper was directed to carry his bride across the threshold of their new home and murmur—using colloquial Japanese—"And now, my pet, I am going to show you a tsingatoo." After one unfortunate showing the "tsingatoo" became plain American "bungalow."

After pictures were completed, we conducted three different types of previews. First comes the honest-to-God preview where a new film is put on cold to get the actual reactions of paying patrons. The behind-the-scenes people who made the picture are the only representatives of the studio in the audience and they check every reaction, every laugh, every indication of appreciation or impatience. Frequently important changes are made in pictures as a consequence of such screenings. I remember, for instance, in *Make Me a Star* (from the book and play, *Merton of the Movies*) how its most touching moment—where the hero prays to God to help him become a good movie actor—was greeted with gales of laughter. Before we had an acceptable movie we had to revise and greatly abbreviate his plea.

Later comes the so-called sneak preview with the theatre carefully packed with strictly studio audiences. Seats are reserved for the big brass and from start to finish the laughter, the tears, the applause, whatever is called for, is deafeningly supplied as if a great new epic were being unveiled. The best place to see these sneak previews, if you hope to retain your self-respect as well as your job, is the seat nearest the door. In this fashion I discovered that I could usually make a speedy exit before I had been buttonholed by the producer or his stooges and forced to pay homage to his incomparable talents.

Last and most trying are the previews de luxe such as we used to hold at Grauman's Chinese Theatre. Klieg lights turn night into day. The streets are jammed with fans. Every important name in Hollywood has to be invited and axes fall if anyone with influence is omitted. As the celebrated arrive and depart they have to be photographed (frequently by newsreel cameras containing no negative). The showing of the film itself is regularly interrupted with tumultuous cheering as each principal makes his or her appearance on the screen. The ovation at the final curtain for everyone important dwarfs the applause for a winning candidate at a political convention; the audience is composed of men and women whose own pictures will be similarly exploited in the not too distant future and they are taking no chances.

· IX ·

THE AUTHOR AND ARCHITECT of Paramount-Publix was the redoubtable Adolph Zukor. What Rockefeller was to oil, Carnegie to steel, Ford to motors, he was—and still is—to movies. I first laid eyes on this deceptively unpretentious little man at a convention of independent exhibitors in Minneapolis in 1921. The avowed purpose of the delegates was to tear him limb from limb for his invasion of the exhibition field. He knew this, but with characteristic courage—he has the heart of a lion in the physique of a chipmunk—he arrived at the scene alone, unexpected and unannounced, and humbly petitioned for the privilege of saying a few words to his would-be lynchers.

His few words lasted several hours. He swore to heaven that the one thing he had never countenanced nor would ever condone was to drive small exhibitors out of business, and if his lieutenants had indulged in such procedures it was unknown to him and contrary to his explicit instructions. Coming from anyone other than Mr. Zukor, this would have sounded as credible as Lizzie Borden's contention that she was in the barn making fishing tackle when the ax fell on her old folks. But he is so plausible a character, in public or private, that when he concluded his remarks the delegates rose en masse in a spontaneous ovation. He answered every accusation (his memory for facts, figures and a little occasional fiction is prodigious); he wept freely (he has a Tennessee Valley control over his tear ducts); and he chose his words with such discretion and skill that his hearers were left with the impression that his theatre acquisition campaign was at an end, although a careful perusal of his words the next morning indicated that he had never said anything of the sort. What he did promise was that he would not acquire theatres in any city where his pictures were being "properly exhibited." The catch consisted in the interpretation of the word "properly" —an interpretation in which Zukor and his customers have rarely agreed.

On a much later occasion, when I was in his employ, I accompanied him to a Paramount convention in Philadelphia where he introduced a representative of the banking firm of Kuhn, Loeb & Company as "a gift from heaven designed to reorganize the company's complicated financial structure." On our way home he freely called the gift from heaven several shorter and earthier names and told me what he intended to do to the Deity's as well as the bankers' spokesman. He did it.

Adolph Zukor arrived in the United States from Hungary in 1888 at the age of fifteen with forty dollars sewed into the lining of his second-best suit. He had been too sick throughout the voyage to undress, which he told me was a blessing; his fellow passengers in the steerage were a hungry crew. On landing he escaped further larceny. In the old days there were hack drivers in New York who made a lively livelihood out of meeting boats and taking immigrants to their destinations by long and circuitous routes. A greenhorn who wanted to go from the Battery to, say, Fourteenth Street, was hospitably taken there via Brooklyn and Queens or by even longer scenic routes, and the fare was frequently his life savings. This reception was called by the ship news reporters of the day "the American welcome." Young Adolph got a free ride on a truck to his destination either through luck or native canniness. I prefer to believe it was the latter.

Orphaned at the age of seven, Adolph was left almost penniless and had to be apprenticed for board and room. Under the law in Hungary at the time, an orphan's inheritance, no matter how small, was administered by the state. Twice a year he had to make out a list of his necessities— a pair of shoes, a hat, a couple of pairs of socks, underwear and any necessary medicines—and this list was sent to his state guardian. Early he noticed that no matter how meager he made his list, it was always pruned. He tried a longer list—three pairs of socks, two hats and four sets of underwear. This list was also pruned but in approximately the same ratio as the first ones, giving Adolph an advantage which increased each time he shrewdly lengthened his list.

Thus early in life he learned the basic principles of motion picture negotiation: ask a lot, settle for less.

His first job upon landing in New York was upholstering sofas for a Second Avenue outfit, but he was so small—he weighed less than a hundred pounds—that he couldn't hold the sofa springs down to tack the batting over them. (No other job outside of holding Mary Pickford down and paying for all the theatres Paramount-Publix acquired ever proved too weighty for him.)

Shortly thereafter he sought to remedy his puniness. He found a boxing instructor, learned how to handle his dukes as creditably as his brain, and in the process acquired a cauliflower ear which throughout his life he has kept close to the ground.

He took his new ear and his new strength into the fur business and prospered sufficiently to lend three thousand dollars to a relative who was operating one of the early peep shows. When it appeared that this investment might be in jeopardy he went into the arcade business to protect it. Never was an investment better protected.

One of Zukor's next ventures was with "Hale's Tours," an early stunt attraction devised and patented by Chief Hale of the Kansas City Fire Department and for which Zukor acquired the New York rights. The "tour" consisted of converting the front of a small store into an imitation of a Pullman car with observation platform. When the seats were occupied, the conductor (and ticket seller) would shout: "All aboard." The car would then start to swing from side to side, rattling realistically, and upon a screen facing the observation platform there appeared moving pic-

"All aboard!"

tures lasting approximately ten minutes, showing scenic marvels such as Mt. Blanc or the Rhine, and giving the travelers the illusion of seeing the wonders of the world.

Hale's repertoire, however, was small, and the beauties of nature and travel were not so compelling as to cause a stampede at the box office. Zukor soon removed the fake car front and the following week with a new front and a new sign reading "Comedy Theatre" he reopened with the "chase" pictures which everyone over fifty will remember. They usually consisted of some miscreant, pursued by a policeman, knocking down, as he ran, a ladder on which a painter was working, whereupon the painter joined in the chase. All three stumbled over a carton of tomatoes and were then followed by an irate grocer encumbered by an umbrella, excitable foreigners, dogs, children and other stray animals. Considering their limited content and their unlimited technical deficiencies, these films did remarkably well for about three years, and certainly they had a vitality and freshness which is rarely found in many more modern and more pretentious productions.

Around 1908 their novelty began to wear off and many exhibitors, deciding that the bloom was off the picture peach, closed up their stores and went back to the circus, or the pants business. The canny and industrious penny arcade owner on Fourteenth Street (who, incidentally, by this time had added to his New York enterprise similar ones in Newark and Philadelphia) was not so easily discouraged. He had made a practice of conducting a nightly poll of his customers, and he was certain that there was nothing wrong with pictures which longer and better ones could not cure. And he was also certain that pictures needed the prestige of famous legitimate actors and actresses.

At that time, however, the Motion Picture Patents Company had an apparently unbreakable grip on all operations of the industry owing to its ownership of the basic Edison patents on all picture-making and picture exhibition equipment. They constituted, and were called, the Trust. Unlike Zukor, they were not in close touch with the public, but like many subsequent leaders of the industry they considered themselves omniscient in knowing what the public wanted. The public had always wanted shorts. It would continue to want them. With wavings of large cigars they further pronounced that the average human mind could not concentrate on pictures running longer than ten minutes. And they forbade the production or exhibition of longer films—what we now call "feature" pictures.

In France, owing to Edison's parsimony in declining to take out foreign patents, there were no restrictions, no trusts and no didactic psychologists. The French producers believed their customers would welcome longer pictures and they made one that ran four reels, or forty minutes. It was *Queen Elizabeth,* whose subsequent showing in America was, as I have already told, to inspire Sam Katz and other ambitious young men. But Zukor did not even have to wait to see it. As soon as he heard about it he realized that this was what he had been looking for—a "feature" picture with the biggest star of the day, Sarah Bernhardt. He sought out the representative of the foreign producer. "How much do you want for the American rights?" he asked. "Thirty-five thousand dollars," was the answer, "half cash." To the amazement of the vendor, who had anticipated considerable agreeable haggling, Zukor answered immediately, "I'll take it."

He had everything but a license to exhibit a long picture. He went to the offices of the Trust, hat in hand, respectfully, to try to beguile the magnates into giving him one. He sat for three hours waiting. Finally he was ushered into the sanctum of the mighty. They were, it appeared, rushing off to an important luncheon appointment and had no time to discuss irrelevancies with little arcade owners. They lived to regret the luncheon. Zukor put on his hat, walked out and decided to show the *Queen* in defiance of the Trust.

He went about it skillfully. He opened an uptown office. The name of his new firm, "Famous Players," and his new slogan, "Famous Players in Famous Plays," was painted on the office door. He then hired some capable helpers. One was Benjamin J. Schulberg, a former newspaperman turned publicity hound, and later to father a lot of successful films as well as two successful sons, Budd and Stuart. Another was Daniel Frohman, the distinguished theatrical producer. Owing to a series of flops, Frohman at the time was long on prestige but short on cash. When approached by Zukor, who knew (probably to the dime) what his financial status was, Frohman unhesitatingly said, "I'm in a venturesome mood." His brother Charles, who was currently profitably impresarioing Maude Adams and James Barrie, could not have been more disgusted, it has been reported, had his brother "opened a hot-dog stand at Coney Island."

146

Through Dan Frohman, Zukor rented a legitimate theatre, the Lyceum, for the showing of *Queen Elizabeth*. On a momentous evening in 1912, he inaugurated the first of the gala openings which have since cast so many Klieg lights on ermine coats and stuffed shirts. New York's most celebrated and powerful were corralled and steered there by Frohman, and their eminent presences and enthusiastic endorsements of the picture were kept no secret by Schulberg. This unexpected rallying by the influential and affluential put the Trust under such pressure that it capitulated and granted Zukor and other producers licenses to make longer films.

Whether it was Zukor who in this manner "broke the Trust," as has been suggested by his official biographer, is highly dubious. There were many personalities involved (among them other rebels like Carl Laemmle and William Fox) and many contributory influences (among them the U. S. courts), but certainly shortly thereafter the Trust dwindled and died, while Zukor blossomed and flourished.

The success of Sarah in *Queen* confirmed Zukor's conviction that picture patrons wanted well-known legitimate players. It was equally clear that some other producer might prematurely arrive at the same conclusion. Moving with his customary speed and courage, he proceeded to sign up James O'Neill, father of Eugene, Minnie Maddern Fiske, Lillie Langtry and a score of others, equally distinguished. With James Hackett in the lead, the new firm of Famous Players produced its first picture, *The Prisoner of Zenda*. Edwin Porter was its director.

Zukor soon discovered, however, that stage stars had

147

their handicaps. They regarded movie making as a menial art unworthy of their talents, one to be undertaken only when they were stone broke. The Edison Company had to build its studio in the Bronx, then a remote New York suburb, so that actors could slip in and out unseen. They also used fictitious names to hide their identities and keep their shame from Broadway. When Dustin Farnum was first approached to star in a movie, he bristled, "What! Go into pictures at the height of my career?" For his remuneration he was offered several thousand dollars' worth of stock in a company which later developed into Paramount Pictures Inc. (When typing the original incorporation papers, a secretary forgot the comma after the word "Pictures," an oversight which has brought many gray hairs to publicity men and newspaper compositors ever since.) Had he taken it, it would today be worth over a million dollars. Instead, he insisted on five thousand dollars in cash, or a buck-in-the-hand deal.

A further peril in dealing with the haughty legitimates proved to be the merciless lens of the camera. It revealed the matinee idol as long past his youth, and the leading ladies' chins and figures as long past theirs. Also, with few exceptions, the early motion picture fans were men and women of modest means who had never been theatregoers and who consequently were little impressed by Zukor's big names. From the first, movie addicts have insisted on selecting their own gods and goddesses and they have seldom appreciated well-lined faces indicative of sensitivity or intelligence as much as magazine cover girls. The success of occasional mature performers like the Barrymores, Leslie

Howard and George Arliss has been an exception to the customary emphasis on youth. Maxine Elliott, Jane Cowl, Ina Claire, Helen Hayes, Lynn Fontanne, Alfred Lunt, Ezio Pinza and others among the stage's great have all failed to achieve widespread movie popularity. Alla Nazimova's films proved so costly in reshootings, lighting, make-up and cutting, and then did so poorly at the box office, that one critic called her "a luxury only America could afford." With a few memorable exceptions, moviedom's great favorites from John Bunny to John Wayne have achieved their fame and fortune on the screen.

Joan Crawford began her triumphant career after winning a Charleston contest. Lana Turner was discovered in a Hollywood drugstore. Gloria Swanson and Marie Prevost were alumnae of Mack Sennett's bathing beauties, and Jean Harlow and Janet Gaynor had their film baptism in Hal Roach's comedies. Charlie Chaplin was so little known when he was first signed up that he was addressed as Charles Chapman. Wallace Beery started his film career by impersonating a Swedish maid.

Fame and fortune were once offered another amateur who passed them up. He was Czar Nicholas. Lewis J. Selznick, the producer, sent Nicholas a cable which read, "When I was poor boy in Kiev some of your policemen were not kind to me and my people. I came to America and prospered. Stop. Now hear with regret you are out of a job. Stop. Feel no ill will over what your policemen did, so if you will come to New York can give you fine position acting in pictures. Stop. Salary no object. Stop. Reply my expense. Stop. Regards you and family." He received no reply.

After his false start with stage stars, Zukor quickly switched to screen stars. The most famous was Mary Pickford. The fact that she was under contract to another producer was irrelevant. He needed her desperately and money, he figured, would talk. America's sweetheart figured the same way. They both figured for weeks. Mopping his brow, Zukor finally and staggeringly met her adamant price. It was the then unheard of salary of twenty thousand dollars a year. Only four years earlier little Gladys Smith had gone to work for D. W. Griffith at Biograph for five dollars a day, and quickly, even in those pre-star days, became fondly known as "Little Mary." Within another four years, Zukor was to be paying her $520,000 annually.

Patience, resourcefulness and a perfect sense of timing have always been Zukor's strong assets and his use of them in handling potential rivals can be adduced from the way he eventually took the cable-sending Mr. Selznick into camp. Selznick entered the business in the early teens and for a dozen years was a sensational figure. His entry itself was indicative of some of the alertness and luck which enabled him to forge ahead so rapidly. Selznick was a jeweler. When he decided to look into the picture business, he called at the Universal offices. Sitting in the waiting room, it became apparent that all was not well with Universal (it rarely has been for any length of time). The offices were a scene of confusion instead of creative activities, and more crowded with process servers than customers.

The heads of the company were at loggerheads with each other and so mutually suspicious that strong-arm men were stationed in the outer offices to search all strangers to see if they packed a gun or a blackjack.

Selznick fortunately had some precious stones on his person and when frisked said he was a jewelry salesman and was allowed to pass. The owners were so absorbed in their private feud that he not only got into an office but hung up his hat and went to work. Not being on speaking terms, the various factions assumed that one of the others had hired the stranger. The new business seemed superlatively adapted to his gifts, so Selznick put himself on the payroll and started to learn all about it. He also appointed himself mediator between the warring forces. This proved his undoing, for it brought the newcomer more forcefully to their attention and when Carl Laemmle finally emerged the winner, as usual, the first thing he did was to fire the conciliator.

Considering himself, however, a thoroughly experienced movie man by this time, Selznick quickly went on to bigger and better things. His two great motivating forces became love of personal publicity and jealousy of Adolph Zukor. With a few stars like Clara Kimball Young and Norma Talmadge, he formed the Selznick Company and it appeared for a time that he might indeed be capable of gratifying his wish and confident prediction that he would "hang Zukor's hide on his door."

Selznick, however, expanded too rapidly and there came a day when he desperately needed some ready cash. Zukor, who usually knew every move made in the industry before it was even a stir, and who, moreover, was frequently himself the behind-the-scenes stirrer, was in no way surprised at Selznick's predicament. And it "just happened" that on the particular day it was he who was in a position to help his rival out with half a million dollars in ready cash for a half interest and a silent partnership in the Selznick Company. Selznick was in no position to reject so gracious an offer.

The silent partner effected a few minor changes. One of them was the disappearance from the firm's title of the name "Selznick," on whose exploitation its owner had lavished so much loving energy and money. Almost overnight the corporation was rechristened Select Pictures. Publicity was bountiful for the firm's pictures and stars, but there seemed to be an increasing fuzziness as to whom they belonged to. Zukor also thought that Select's films would prove more profitable if they were of a cheaper brand than those made by his own Famous Players-Lasky Company. He was right. Exhibitors who could not afford to buy his high-priced product readily rented the comparatively inexpensive Select pictures. The changes effected gave Zukor profit and pleasure. They gave Selznick profit and pain. In due time Zukor permitted him to buy back his half interest. For one million dollars.

A free man once more, Selznick promptly changed the firm name to Selznick Select and added the slogan "Selznick Pictures Make Happy Hours." He renewed his campaign for Zukor's hide and again began to predict that the trophy would soon be his, and this time in shreds.

Around the corner from these boasts another company

magically appeared, specializing in almost the same type of pictures and employing many former members of the Selznick distributing organization. It was called Realart and offered such attractions to its customers as Bebe Daniels, Mary Miles Minter, Constance Binney and others. Realart was ostensibly an independent company but it did not take long for the rumor to spread that it was privately owned by Mr. Zukor. Certainly it was in direct competition with Selznick, and it was discontinued only when all danger from that gentleman had disappeared.

Eventually Selznick went into a less speculative business, Florida real estate. His two able sons, however, were destined to remain in Hollywood and add fresh laurels to the Selznick name. Myron became head of one of the leading theatrical agencies. David is the producer of some of the greatest successes in movie history, among them *Gone With the Wind* and *Duel in the Sun*.

Four years after Zukor had humbly appeared before the Trust he was himself rapidly assuming the dimensions of a monopoly. The obscure investor of three thousand dollars in a penny arcade had become the head of Famous Players-Lasky Corporation, a twenty-five-million-dollar combination, the largest producer and distributor of motion pictures in the world. More than half the best-known screen performers were on his payroll. To secure the pictures in which they appeared, exhibitors had to rent all of Zukor's other films. On all of these, good and bad, he regularly increased the rentals and when exhibitors refused to accede to his terms he acquired competitive theatres in their towns. There was little fear in exhibitor circles of other producers such as William Fox, and genuine affection for Marcus Loew and Carl Laemmle, but by 1917 the battle cry of theatre owners from coast to coast was, to paraphrase it politely, "Stop Zukor."

As usual, a crisis created leaders. One was Thomas Tally, by then an important Los Angeles exhibitor. Another was J. D. Williams, a former treasurer of the Parkersburg, West Virginia, Opera House, who had acquired a reputation as a truculent go-getter in the Australian movie world. Williams barnstormed the country urging American exhibitors to stop being saps, to pool their purchasing power and to deal directly with the stars instead of through Zukor or any other intermediary. Twenty-seven major theatre circuit owners, who had previously rarely agreed on anything, responded with alacrity to what sounded to them like common sense. Representing over one hundred theatres in thirty-five key cities, they became the charter stock owners of First National Exhibitors Circuit. Every stockholder owned the franchise for his territory. Each agreed to pay his proportionate share of the costs of film production and to sell subfranchises to neighborhood theatres and those in smaller towns. In this fashion First National was adequately financed and in a comparatively short time included approximately six thousand exhibitors.

To line up the stars it needed for its program, First National, dominated by theatre owners who had always castigated Zukor for the high salaries he paid, immediately proceeded to offer salaries the like of which had never before been known in the movies or in any other industry. They wangled Chaplin from Mutual for $1,075,000. He was hired to make eight pictures annually, supposedly two-reelers, as he had never made a long picture. Chaplin soon surprised his new employers in a most agreeable fashion by turning out his first and enormously successful feature film, *The Kid.*

With Chaplin as a shining example, First National lured other stars, all at substantially increased salaries, into their fold: among them the Talmadge sisters, Lionel Barrymore, Anita Stewart, Katherine MacDonald, as well as Thomas H. Ince with his fine production facilities. Zukor, however, still held the ace, Mary Pickford. Benjamin Hampton in his *History of the Movies* was not guilty of overstating the situation when he wrote, "Although theatres, studios and exchanges in 1917-18 represented investments of several millions of dollars and gave employment to a hundred thousand people, Mary Pickford remained the industry's most valuable asset. Woman's place in business has grown enormously in importance in the last three decades, but Mary Pickford is the only member of her sex who ever became the focal point of an entire industry. Her position was unique; probably no man or woman will ever again win so extensive a following." Certainly no other woman was ever able to remark coyly to her employer, "But I can't afford to work for only ten thousand dollars a week."

Regardless of cost, First National—if it was going to drive the monopolistic Zukor out of business and establish its own monopoly—had to have Mary. Zukor, through Artcraft, one of his camouflaged outfits, was paying her $520,000 annually with an additional bonus based on her pictures' profits. Williams et al offered her $1,050,000 for three pictures. Mary said "No." Chaplin, a comparative Johnny-Come-Lately, was doing better than that. Eventually, it was agreed to pay Mama Pickford $50,000 for her "good offices and good wishes," so that Mary, by a narrow margin, could shade Charlie.

Unable to see where even Pickford was worth so fabulous a sum, Zukor made one last effort to keep her from deserting to First National. "You've worked very hard for years," he told her. "Why don't you take a vacation? If you will stop making pictures for five years, I will give you two hundred and fifty thousand dollars."

"Oh, I couldn't do that, Mr. Zukor," she answered. "I love pictures, and I'm just a girl. I couldn't quit now."

In spite of Mary's defection, Zukor still had great stars in his stable like Doug Fairbanks, Sr., Bill Hart, Tom Meighan, Pauline Frederick, Blanche Sweet, the rapidly rising Gloria Swanson; also the famous director, D. W. Griffith. But in 1918 a palace revolt as dangerous to his old regime as to First National's new one broke out. The inventors had sought to establish a trust through the control of patents, Zukor through the use of famous players in famous stories, the exhibitors through the control of brick and mortar. Now the stars (with some prompting by ex-Zukor henchmen like Schulberg and Hy Abrams, his former production and sales chiefs) decided that the movie firmament revolved about them. If First National could afford to pay millions for their services why should they not make and distribute their own product and retain all of the profits that were being appropriated by greedy entrepreneurs such as the producers and the exhibitors?

Again there were high-voltage scurryings, midnight conferences, name callings and figurings on the back of envelopes. They gave birth in 1919 to a new company, United Artists, headed by the industry's three supreme box-office bets—Mary Pickford, Douglas Fairbanks, Sr. (whom Mary married), and Charlie Chaplin—as well as D. W. Griffith. When Richard Rowland, president of Metro, heard the news, he aptly epitomized the reaction of most of the picture world by remarking, "The lunatics have taken charge of the asylum."

With exhibitors and stars vigorously asserting their interests, Zukor was no man to stand by twiddling his thumbs. Divide and conquer was a history book maxim with which he was well acquainted and which he knew how to apply to perfection. Soon United Artists was torn by internal dissensions. D. W. Griffith, dissatisfied with his treatment by his partners, returned to the Paramount lot. In 1924 Fairbanks produced *The Thief of Bagdad* for the then-fabulous sum of two million dollars. After deducting distribution charges it barely returned its original investment. Mary Pickford did a Brodie when she attempted to depart from her sweet little girl roles in *Dorothy Vernon of Haddon Hall*. Apparently it was not so easy to make profits in the new role of producers and distributors as the stars had assumed.

First National was even more susceptible than United Artists both to direct attack and subtle infiltration. Early in 1919 Zukor answered the exhibitor challenge by acquir-

ing a stranglehold on Broadway through the purchase of
the Rivoli and Rialto Theatres. As yet there was no Roxy
or Music Hall so only the Strand was left available to play
First National and the Capitol to play Metro. The story,
as Zukor himself tells it, of how he made this deal is characteristic of the man and his method of transacting business.

"I sent for the owners of these two theatres and told
them we would like to make arrangements to book our
pictures in their theatres. They hesitated because they
were thinking of the high prices they had to pay for our
pictures. I think we charged them one thousand dollars a
week. We are getting fifteen thousand dollars a week now.
Finally, they made a proposition to sell the theatres, which
was just what I wanted. I said, 'I'll buy, if the price is right.'
The man with whom I was talking took out a pencil and
figured how much preferred stock they had outstanding
and how much common stock and said, 'We will sell the
common stock at fifty-five dollars a share.' I do not know
to this day how many shares he had, but I grabbed him by
the hand and said, 'All right, I will take them.' "

He also proceeded to deal effectively with First National
in Los Angeles by purchasing Grauman's Million Dollar
and the Rialto. In the meantime, he quietly acquired an
interest in the Stanley Company of Philadelphia and the
Saenger Amusement Company of New Orleans, the two
most powerful circuits in America, both charter members
of First National. Another First National stalwart was
Hulsey, a leading circuit owner of Texas and Oklahoma.
Hulsey, though prosperous, had overexpanded and was in

debt to his bank. One day that bank received a deposit of one million dollars to the credit of Southern Enterprises, the name under which Lynch and Paramount conducted their theatre activities in the South. In those prehistoric days a million dollars sounded like a lot of money in Dallas. The worried banker told Hulsey that he had better make the best terms possible with Zukor—and Hulsey did what he was told.

As part of Zukor's strategy, this deal was not publicized and for many months First National could not ascertain whether or not Hulsey had deserted. Uncertainty bred consternation. As Tally put it, "If Hulsey has been licked and is keeping quiet about it, how many more of our stockholders are really Zukor's representatives at our board meetings?"

By 1921 Zukor was in control of some four hundred well-located theatres and negotiating for others. His product, in spite of the loss of Mary and Doug, was still tops and in nation-wide demand. The threat of both First National and United Artists to Paramount's supremacy had been safely surmounted.

Even in the bitterest of these battles, Zukor showed outwardly few symptoms of the pressure and excitement under which he worked. Only occasionally, in righteous wrath, have I heard him raise his voice at the strange reluctance of some people to let him be the leader. He may not always have conducted himself according to the Marquess of Queensberry rules, but he invariably observed the precepts of correct etiquette as decreed by Emily Post. Indeed, on one occasion I received a wire from him reading, "You are herewith discharged same to take effect immediately stop. Best regards."

He once opened a school on the Paramount lot where young actresses under contract to the company were taught how to walk, sit, speak and what to speak about. They were given classes in sociology and English literature and lectured on all the proprieties, including chastity.

Many unkind things have been said about him in the heat of conflict but although he has spent unlimited hours in the company of the loveliest and least discreet of ladies, no one has even suggested that he was engaged in pursuits other than those of a strictly business nature. It is true that he scarcely looks like a Lothario, but many of his confreres, equally inadequately endowed by nature for the part, have taken advantage of their power, for seductive purposes. Never Zukor, or if Zukor, never indiscreetly.

On one occasion a widely read columnist published a rumor that the Zukors were contemplating a separation. This was the only occasion in all the years that I knew him, and in all the attacks made upon him, that he asked me personally to see that a story was denied. He was solicitous that his wife should not be involved in what such a rumor meant to him—"a public scandal."

I recall one time after we had prepared all the advertising for a picture entitled *The Woman Who Needed Killing*, Zukor insisted that the title must be changed. It seemed to him to imply a slur on womanhood and we had to remake all of the publicity accessories rather than give the impression that Paramount was in any degree lacking in respect for America's wives and mothers. The new title was *A Dangerous Woman*.

When Roscoe Arbuckle became involved in a squalid episode culminating in the death of a young girl at a wild hotel party, Zukor did not hesitate. Although Fatty was one of the most profitable Paramount stars with over a million dollars invested in his films, Zukor immediately ordered: "Stop work on current Arbuckle film and withdraw all prints from circulation." "For how long?" asked his sales chief. "Forever," answered Zukor. Although vindicated later at his trial, neither the public nor Zukor ever again found the fat man funny.

He practiced the open-door policy, and even on his busiest days was always approachable. In this respect he differed strongly from some of his lieutenants. For example, while *The Ten Commandments* was being made, Theodore Roberts and James Neil in their biblical costumes stopped off to see the director, Cecil DeMille. They sat in his outer office for what seemed an interminable time and finally sent in word—"Moses and Aaron are still waiting to see God."

In spite of his financial success, Zukor always remained a singularly modest and unassuming man. When he was given a dinner at the opening of the new Paramount Building, all he could be persuaded to say was, "This is not a monument dedicated to me, as some of you gentlemen have suggested, but rather a monument to an America which could give a chance to a boy like me to be connected with an institution like this."

The same night, before the first invited guest arrived,

he stood in the theatre lobby, a strangely small figure cast against the giant stairway, the gargantuan chandeliers and the numerous nymphs in ormolu. "Maybe it is not good enough," he kept saying. "Maybe we ought to have spent more to make sure that everything was just right." Personally I never thought it was good enough, but Otto Kahn came along and said it was. Zukor relaxed. The Maecenas of the Arts had spoken.

When the Paramount Building and Theatre opened in 1926 the twenty-five-million-dollar combination of 1916 had expanded to a net worth of 149 million. For the next four years its career continued to be sensationally successful. It seemed immune to the nation-wide business collapse of 1929 and that year made $15,544,000. In 1930 it was almost three million dollars more. We smugly told ourselves that people might economize on groceries or clothes but not on entertainment and that ours was a depression-proof industry. In 1932 we learned to the contrary. In that year, Paramount-Publix (the new corporate name) lost close to $16,000,000.

The company might, however, like Loew's and Warners, have escaped bankruptcy but the straw that broke the octopus' back was its obligations on its own stock.

In the Publix stampede for theatres, some genius, over Zukor's protest, I am told, had evolved a marvelous scheme for solving the ancient dilemma of what happens when an irresistible force meets an immovable body. If an exhibitor demanded $8,000,000 for his circuit and Paramount could not see its way clear to offer more than $6,000,000, he was paid off with the company's stock, then selling at

60, but with a so-called repurchase clause at $80 a share. In this fashion, predicated on the popular theory of the twenties that the stock market would always continue to rise, both buyer and seller were satisfied. Unfortunately, by 1932 the financial honeymoon was over and the vendor who was then entitled to $8,000,000 held stock worth only about $2,000,000. Paramount-Publix owed him the difference but it was in no position to pay that difference. It owned some 1700 pieces of real estate with a value upwards of $216,000,000, but its outstanding obligations amounted to approximately $70,000,000. Long before the situation became publicly known it would have been possible for Zukor, with a little deft manipulation, personally to have escaped from the debacle with comparatively minor losses. He chose to go down with his ship.

The company was reorganized and Zukor was demoted upstairs to Chairman of the Board. Katz's resignation was accepted. In due time he associated himself with Metro-Goldwyn-Mayer, a company which both before and after his arrival has been celebrated for relying less on scientific business management and more on hunch and intuition than any other in the industry. These methods, it might be added, under the leadership of Nicholas Schenck, have made it consistently successful.

After the reorganization, several presidents for Paramount were trotted out. The right man was finally found and still has the job—Barney Balaban. Steve Lynch, whose aggressive tactics had originally brought so many of the theatres into the company's fold, was drafted to reorganize their operation. For most of them partnerships were formed

with the "robber barons" who had originally owned them
—with the wise and caustic Bob Wilby in the Southwest,
the hard-fisted, hard-headed Richards in Louisiana and
Mississippi, the studious, reserved Hoblitzelle in Texas. In
their experienced, tough hands and with the blessings of
local control and reduced overhead that ensued from the
prompt discharge of all of the Publix experts, the new
setup became more profitable than ever, until, as a result
of the court decree, exhibition was eventually divorced
from production and distribution activities. A new circuit,
the largest in the world, United Paramount Theatres, was
established, under the leadership of a new type of movie
magnate, Leonard Goldenson, a Harvard graduate and a
lawyer by training, who runs his organization with less
guesswork and overnight decisions than the pioneers and
with less home office dictation and strict supervision than
Katz.

The years and some adversity have chastened and mel-
lowed Adolph Zukor. Newcomers find him "gentle" and
"kindly" and susceptible ladies call him "too sweet for
words." They should see him in action as I did only recently. A critical issue had arisen. A meeting attended by
all the companies' top executives was held. There was the
usual orating and the usual clash of opinion. Then "the
old man," as we now call him, arose. With all of his old
fire and clarity of vision he analyzed the problem and urged
a decisive and courageous course of action. "Stop Zukor,"
the exhibitors and his competitors used to cry. I have still
to find anybody who could do it.

· X ·

AFTER A COUPLE OF YEARS at Paramount of interrupted sleep and crisping arteries (my blood pressure rose every time my advertising budget was lowered), I began to lose my enthusiasm for the daily hagglings with executives, space salesmen and actors. I began to wonder what life was like on the outside, and to consider some enterprise suitable for a reasonably sane man. Businesses like hay and oats began to appeal to me, as did twine and hardware and chicken raising; even pool parloring, horse currying and marriage brokering began to look greener to me than movie advertising, and I might have chosen one of those pastures —at one point operating a race track was suggested and it seemed a comparatively serene career—but opportunity knocked my door down and I remained in the movie business.

Spies reported to me that Paramount was losing so much money at its Rialto Theatre in New York that it was preparing to default on the lease and return the property to its owner. When I heard this news I knew immediately that what I really wanted was a theatre of my own, to operate as I wanted, to play the pictures I wanted and to advertise them the way I wanted. The Rialto was, in short, exactly what I wanted. (I had not yet learned that next to not getting what you want, the greatest disappointment in life is to get what you want.) Consequently and quickly, I offered to swap Paramount my long-term contract for its Rialto lease. I thought they would consider any offer appealing which would relieve them of the Rialto, but the alacrity with which they jumped at my canceled contract was downright unflattering.

Before we knew quite what had happened to us, the Rialto and I found ourselves out of the parent company and on the sidewalk at Forty-second Street and Broadway —the crossroads of the world—with a parental blessing and little else. Some people, incidentally, think the Rialto is on Seventh Avenue but among its many other absurdities, Broadway actually has six corners where it intercepts Forty-second Street, four on the north side and two on the south, a setup which, after I took up residence there, inspired a nettled competitor of mine to rechristen it the double crossroads of the world. Anyhow, Paramount closed the doors of the Rialto one day. I reopened them the next.

That next was March 4, 1933—the day the banks closed. There wasn't one loose buck on Broadway, but undaunted, I ordered that anyone lacking cash should be

admitted to the theatre in return for an IOU, and a six-
foot notice was posted outside to that effect. Business was
sensational. I would not go so far as to say that my first
day in business disillusioned me as to the innate honesty
of mankind, but for the protection of future optimists I
should report that only a small percentage of the IOU's
was ever redeemed. My deal with Paramount had not yet
been signed when I opened, but that rare amalgam of
attorney and sage, Leo Spitz, who was at the time conducting the company's complicated affairs (and recently
executive head of production at Universal Pictures), suggested that if I wanted to operate the theatre before I
stumbled over my long gray beard, I had better proceed
without waiting around for the final legal technicalities to
be conclusively settled. Even a Spitz could not foresee the
grave error which I committed. I took the Rialto out of the
red immediately.

It required no miracle man to accomplish this. I merely
cut a five-thousand-dollar weekly advertising budget to less
than five hundred dollars; I canceled the "free list" (the
house seated two thousand people but four thousand politicians, bankers and friends of the former management had
the privilege of entering any time they pleased); and I reduced the service staff, or rather, heaved most of it over-
board, as the place was bristling with overpaid West Point-
trained ushers instructing customers kindly to expectorate
only into the sand-filled Grecian urns. I replaced them with
genial, slouchy, underpaid boys, the most underpaid being
my son, Michael. I got him cheap, owing to his innocence
about money matters, but before he finally discarded his

usher's uniform, he had wised up alarmingly. He turned out to be an excellent usher and developed such diplomacy that for a while I had ideas about trying to get him a job at the Court of St. James', like Ambassador or something. One of my pleasantest memories of the Rialto was sitting in the dark there one day looking at a Washington newsreel (in which I appeared for three seconds. I sat through the reel every day for a week just to catch those three seconds), when I heard Michael approach and address an overly amorous couple next to me. "If you don't mind, sir," he said, "would you kindly transfer your activities to the balcony? It's rather empty there today and I think you will enjoy the added privacy."

I gave him a fifty-cent raise that week. He held out for seventy-five.

When apprised of the fact that the Rialto was back on its feet in so short a time, the startled Paramount trustees began to reconsider their approval of my sublease and it was only through Spitz's spirited intervention that a compromise was eventually arranged by which my interest in the house was reduced to only 50 per cent, together with a management contract. Those flashy though meager profits of my first few weeks as an entrepreneur cost me half a million dollars.

My shotgun Paramount partnership lasted three years until the original Rialto lease expired, when the landlord insisted on reconstructing the theatre without a balcony and with the number of seats reduced from two thousand to six hundred. Again Paramount was convinced (and again incorrectly) that the Rialto was hopeless. This time

I waited until the decision was signed, sealed and notarized and then I proceeded, with the assistance of a few old friends like the debonair Dembow, to negotiate a new twenty-year lease.

My first concern after cutting the Rialto budget had been how to get pictures. The distributor-owned Broadway houses, stretching from Forty-third Street to Fifty-first, had all the best product sewed up. I could not compete against them with left-over second-rate musicals, routine love stories and polite, innocuous comedies unbuttressed by celebrated stars, or with bright kiddie features minus Deanna Durbin or Mickey Rooney. The only other type of B pictures consistently available to an independent operator like myself was the M product—mystery, mayhem and murder. From hunger, and not acumen, I began to buy these rejects, and shortly to specialize in them.

For fifteen years no Rialto audience ever heard any sophisticated drawing-room chatter or saw men fencing in doublet and hose or listened to a coloratura soprano or watched a lady's bosom gently pant with tender romance; our ladies' bosoms were designed exclusively as targets for daggers or gats. And when an arm was slipped around a lady's waist in seeming amorousness, a close-up would quickly reveal that the hand on the end of that arm was a vampire's claw. In our newsreels, we consistently eliminated the fashion items, the Mardi Gras celebration in New Orleans and the baby parade at Ocean City, New Jersey. Our short features were chiefly prizefight and low comedy pictures, and no Rialto patron was ever transported to a far-distant isle of romance to leave it in sad farewell as the sun slowly sank on its beautiful shores.

Across the street, the New Amsterdam Theatre, under Flo Ziegfeld, had once declared that its ideal was to glorify the American girl. Ours was to gorify the American ghoul and to that end we did our best to remain dedicated and devout. Our telephone operator was instructed to answer all incoming calls with weekly variations of "Help, murder, police! This is the Rialto, now playing *Dracula*, best thriller of the year," which she did with clarion conscientiousness until the city authorities gagged her. I became known up and down Broadway as the Merchant of Menace, and I achieved the Broadway equivalent of immortality when it was printed in a newspaper gossip column one day that Sam Goldwyn had said, "When I see the pictures they play in that theatre it makes the hair stand on the edge of my seat." It was a delicate compliment and I saw to it that it was reprinted and reprinted. (Its true author was, I am told, the Hollywood director, Mike Curtiz.) We were not officially launched, however, until *The New York Times* summed up one year's record with, "No hits, no runs, just terrors."

Among others who properly appreciated the Rialto was Jascha Heifitz, the eminent violinist, with whom I made one of the most unfair arrangements ever consummated— occasional tickets to his marvelous concerts in return for a Rialto season pass.

Only five basic plots furnished the formulae from which 90 per cent of our pictures were constructed, but when I occasionally felt cramped and handicapped by the limited

The Merchant of Menace takes over the Rialto.

fare, I would recall Owen Davis, who consistently wrote about twenty melodramas a year. When asked how he could maintain such a high productivity, he said, "It's easy. I have a good plot." Our plots, roughly summarized, were:

Mad scientist labors in his test-tube-packed laboratory for reasons never fully elucidated, but which would interest his psychoanalyst, to transform lovely young things into gruesome monsters, but even his devoted hunchback retainer cannot save him from the wrath of the local villagers, led by the loveliest young thing's lustiest young man; and the picture ends in a crescendo of burning buildings, burning kisses and the burning shrieks of the experimenter as he is devoured by his experiments.

Newspaper reporter is included among the mourners on the stormy night when the old family lawyer reads the will to the expectant heirs gathered in the cobweb-covered old manse and it is he, rather than the baffled police sergeant (comic relief), who detects that the eminent anthropologist with the dark glasses, to all appearances the most innocent of the inmates, is trying to deprive the enchanting heroine of her inheritance by driving her mad with green hands emerging from secret panels, winking portraits, skeletons in every closet and the murder of the sinister butler, not to mention six equally offensive but guiltless relatives.

Handsome, hard-knuckled local boy makes good, fighting his way through a rapid series of knockout montages to the championship, throws over the little woman and the canny manager who had been his inspiration in his early hardships, falls for a brittle upper-crust babe, indulges in wild orgies of drinking, dancing and petting, and, as the inevitable consequence, is on the floor for the final count when he spies his quondam girl waving encouragement to him as she and his ex-manager rush down the aisle, whereupon he leaps to his feet, reels for half a reel about the ring, and then, with his mighty old-time one-two, fells his adversary and retains his championship.

Tough, inarticulate sergeant and serpent-tongued corporal meet in every quarter of the globe and give each other no quarter in the pursuit of their quarry, but in spite of all the opprobrious epithets they would have hurled at each other if undeterred by the Legion of Decency, they stand shoulder to shoulder when the native drums start to beat, the signal fires are flaming across the hills, and the platoon is preserved from slaughter only by their courage and ingenuity until the photo-finish arrival of reinforcements guided across a secret mountain pass by the current native recipient of their attentions, who, in the final fade-out, is using her hips devastatingly on a dewy-eyed second lieutenant while the non-coms continue their battle.

Brash OSS man parachutes into hostile territory, baffles the Gestapo, blows up most of Germany's airplanes, munition dumps and strategic bridges while pursued by five thousand Storm Troopers, raids Nazi headquarters at midnight to decipher their code, thus saving Patton's army and the entire British fleet, not to mention the intrepid girl leader of the resistance movement who proves to be a member of New York's café society. (This was a perennial, but it had to be refurbished occasionally to the extent of substituting our allies for our former enemies.)

In an effort to pick out the most desirable of these available plots, I used to screen on an average two pictures a day, or over six hundred a year. Prior to my entry into the field, the record for looking at films had been established by former President Gómez of Venezuela, who, in his prime, was the world's most indefatigable moviegoer, his record being 350 a year. In his spare time, however, he fathered over a hundred children, a record which I had neither the opportunity nor the capacity to challenge.

With my limited budget I had little money to spend on newspaper advertising, so I was forced to use the theatre front and the lobby for my major shilling. I removed the marble stairway from the lobby along with a truckload of genuine simulated Renaissance angels; I tossed out the genuine simulated marble busts of Beethoven and Grieg, the perfume machines, and a gallery of paintings of cows grazing in meadows. I replaced these objects of art with fire-snorting, eye-rolling gargoyles, third-degree instruments of torture, a barrel labeled "Beware, Dynamite," papier-mâché fists clenching bloodstained clubs and a poster of a beautiful woman writhing under a sadist's whip—a work which hung next to the American flag that rippled over the whole display, animated by a wind machine. The result may not have been what my mother would have liked, but it pleased my patrons.

When we played a picture called *The Jungle Princess* we re-created a tropical kingdom in the lobby (if re-created is the word and if Nature will pardon me) full of mangy lions, moth-eaten tigers, gaudy, beady-eyed birds, and live monkeys swinging from papier-mâché cocoanut trees. An added sound effect of a lion roaring—so loud it could be heard two blocks away over heavy Broadway traffic—was, I thought, an imaginative touch in a blood-curdling way, but the Police Department felt differently about it and I had to throttle my king of the jungle down to the anemic purr of a superannuated lion (not to be confused with the roar of M-G-M's Leo). The Police Department's tender ears, in fact, remained a constant menace to our sound attractions. Nevertheless, we kept trying. When we played *Homicide Bureau* we called no inconsiderable attention to it with the staccato bark of machine guns, and for Laurel and Hardy and other comedies we prepared a laugh record which gave the impression to passers-by that the audience inside was in spasms. For Laurence Stallings' *First World War*, I ordered the martial music of all nations. My order was too meticulously carried out. I arrived at the theatre on opening day to hear the strains of the Nazi "Horst Wessel" being blared up and down Broadway for blocks. On that occasion I beat the police to its source.

For *The Mummy* we built a colossal and terrifying character combining the most repulsive features of Frankenstein's Monster and Dracula and installed in his insides an electrical device which vibrated waves of alternating crimson and orange from his belly to his brain. We surrounded him with added touches of color and sparks, and a sound effect of grunts came out of his aboriginal jaws. We named him Karloff. Jack McManus, then a film critic on *The New York Times*, commented in print that the show staged outside of the Rialto was far more entertaining than the one inside. In appreciation of his appreciation, we sent him Karloff as a gift. Karloff proved too big even for *The New*

York Times. The elevator bearing him up to McManus' office got stuck with him between floors, snarled up the cables in the adjoining elevators, and for over an hour indignant *Times* personnel had to use the stairs while Karloff was being chopped up. McManus never received our token because after wrestling with him at such length the superintendent of *The Times* building got so mad he threw him out for garbage. *Times* notices of Rialto shows were markedly cool for several weeks thereafter. To add insult to injury, twenty-four hours after this incident a Brooklyn exhibitor called us up, said he had seen and admired Karloff in our lobby, and when we were through with him would we sell him to his theatre for five hundred dollars?

Handicapped by weak casts, the titles of pictures we played assumed even more importance than ordinarily. *A Son Comes Home* was by itself too innocuous to attract patrons, so on the marquee we added *From Gangland.* We strengthened *Fit for a King* by inserting the word *Murder* ahead of it. We were playing *Hollywood Boulevard* when a well-known movie actress achieved notoriety through the tabloid publication of her diary—an impressive tally of her daily indiscretions. We converted the title to the more timely *Hollywood Diary.* Paramount bought the Broadway hit, *Sailor Beware,* and tried to sapolio the story to satisfy the requirements of the Hays Code. (One of the changes was that the girl who couldn't say no to any sailor was switched to a girl who couldn't say yes to anybody.) Eventually, Paramount had to discard what little was left of its original investment, and enforced honesty caused a change of the title to *Lady Behave.* Feeling ourselves under no such obligation to society, we opened the picture on a Friday night as the well-known *Sailor Beware* and enjoyed one week-end of phenomenal business before Paramount, the Motion Picture Association, the Broadway Association, and the original author caught up with us. (No outfit under Barney Balaban's management, however, is likely to waste an asset. Only recently Paramount salvaged a part of its investment in *Sailor Beware*. The old title was dragged out, dusted off and a remote version of the original story was tacked on to it, and the team of Martin and Lewis was engaged to substitute its own routines for most of the remote version.)

We did little newspaper advertising, mainly because of our budget, but when we did, we produced some well-turned prose. "The hand of horror pierces the veil of the spirit world" is a sample. "How would you like to see your own burial?" was attention-getting though it had little connection with the picture it advertised. "Doctor, not that" was used to give an inkling of the content of *Once to Every Woman*, but it proved so popular that we tacked it on to several other pictures, including *River Gang* and *The Cat People* in neither of which any character had ever in his life consulted a doctor, not even a veterinarian. It was in connection with newspaper advertising that my faith in questionnaires was shaken. I instigated one which asked what paper had persuaded the patron to attend the theatre. Most of the answers mentioned a paper in which no Rialto ad had appeared.

From the days when pictures such as *The Great Train Robbery, Trapped by Bloodhounds, U.S. Battleships at*

Sea, custard pie comedies, and other virile fodder were dethroned by the Mary Pickfords, the *Daddy Long Legs* and all the other subsequent "box of candy" pictures and heroines, Hollywood has proceeded on the theory that women like sweetness, light and tender romance. Since Papa goes where Mama goes or Papa don't go out in this country, they have played up to Mama's tastes. Francis X. Bushman's refined love-making replaced Broncho Billy's fast shootin' and hard ridin'—which, incidentally, was a feat in camouflage, inasmuch as Billy was a cowboy right out of the Bronx who never saw a horse in his life until he saw his double riding one. The hunted and bearded villain tracked down by bloodhounds to his hiding place in a muddy, swampy river-bed gave way to the marcelled heroine in a DeMille swan-prowed bed, and the long chase, alas, was replaced by the chaise longue. The saccharine and respectable were enthroned and as Dexter Fellowes, sage of the circus, later said, "Woe betide a generation that prefers Errol Flynn to Buffalo Bill."

The type of picture we featured was rated strictly masculine fare. I considered it that myself and felt for a while like a male suffragette crusading for the privileges and rights of my downtrodden sex. It was a source of gratification, morally and financially, to see so many male patrons assert themselves by patronizing the Rialto and not meekly following their women into the Valentino traps operated by my competitors. We had the most successful three weeks in our history when the male bookers of the Music Hall passed up *The Lost Patrol* because it had no women in the cast and, naturally, no romance. We made Broadway history by double-featuring *Dracula* and *Frankenstein*. Previously, theatre bookers had always assumed that desirable movie entertainment required a well-balanced bill— comedy with romance, or adventure with music—but we jammed the Rialto for several weeks with these two old horror films that had formerly played every shooting gallery in town. Incidentally, this was our only violation of one of our pet slogans, "Not such a good picture, but only *one.*"

For several years my clientele remained largely and defiantly male. And I was informed by my gloating house manager that practically every notorious gangster in New York was included in it. I rarely met these gentlemen as they always patronized the 2:00 A.M. or the 5:00 A.M. show. On a couple of occasions when I stayed up that late, I had to listen to their courteous complaints about our holding shows over too frequently. This, they pointed out, upset their routine of spending one early morning a week at the movies, and they did not like their routines upset. I promised to watch it. In an effort to satisfy them as well as for fairly obvious other reasons, I attempted to jam as many patrons into one week as possible and inaugurated the practice of frequently staying open all night. This attracted many patrons who, for personal reasons, preferred to avoid the more populated hours.

In time, however, to our consternation, feminine attendance started to zoom. Whether this proved that women are not as tender as advertised and as Hollywood still believes, or whether they finally could no longer stand the idea that men were having a good time without them, I do not know. Certainly they were not attracted to the

Rialto by its décor or comforts, but I can honestly report that during the prizefight pictures there could be heard more feminine than masculine voices in the darkness yelling, "Hit him with the right," "Kill the bum," and other such expressions of maidenly advice.

By accident and by degrees the Rialto developed a distinctive personality. At Hollywood conferences, the M pictures began to be referred to as Rialto-type pictures. *The New York Times* wrote glowingly about us, "In its latest metamorphosis, the Rialto has become a cinematic chamber of horrors. Even a casual passer-by is apt to have his wits dislodged by sudden, unearthly sounds from a marquee loud-speaker, or a quick faintness may pass over him when looking up from the baseball scores he sees a desiccated face staring down from a lobby display. Within, the ghosts walk, dead men tell no tales and the darkness is punctuated with the flash of pistol play. Wraiths, Frankensteins, zombies and other mystical bric-a-brac flicker across the screen; things, madmen and fiendish scientists do devilish deeds. In the field of jitters, the Rialto is undoubtedly tops. A goose pimple is its trademark. If old Oscar Hammerstein could see it today, it would set him clawing at his shrouds."

The old Hammerstein referred to was Oscar I, who built opera houses all over the world and who was the grandfather of the current Oscar II, who co-authored *Rose-Marie, Show Boat, The Desert Song, Oklahoma, South Pacific, The King and I*, and also, I think, *La Traviata, Die Meistersinger, Tristan und Isolde, Madame Butterfly, Pagliacci, Iolanthe* and *Pirates of Penzance*, although it is possible that I am thinking of a couple of other fellows. Nevertheless, his grandfather built the Rialto in 1898 and christened it the Victoria, because, as he said at the time, "I have been victorious over my enemies." It remained the Victoria until 1916. On its roof he built a small farm, lived there for a while himself and kept some assorted livestock, including a cow. This "farm in the middle of Manhattan" could be seen at certain hours of the day by visitors for an admittance fee, and it was how I first saw the theatre. Grandpa took me there as a gawky boy in knee pants and it was there that I first saw a cow milked. I was much impressed by the sight, little dreaming that I would ever grow up to be accused one day of milking that same corner myself. Before Hammerstein, Broadway and Forty-second Street—which also housed a garish dance hall—was not a corner where you would expect to find your little sister, and the site of the Victoria itself had been occupied by the Market Stables. During my residence at the Rialto, more than one long-memoried critic recalled nostalgically that the old neighborhood odors had been pleasanter.

Although built by Oscar I, the managing genius of the Victoria was, without doubt, the never-to-be-forgotten Willie Hammerstein, father of Oscar II. And if *The New York Times* thought I was responsible for ghouling up the corner, I would like to point out at this late date that I was only carrying on a carbon copy of the tradition established there by Willie. Compared to Willie, I was St. Francis of Assisi.

The Victoria was built and advertised as a home for "a new form of family entertainment" and it was indeed the forerunner of the vaudeville type of theatre, such as the Palace, but among its family-type entertainment acts, introduced by Willie, were Ethel Conrad and Lillie Graham, an attractive brace of girls who could not sing, dance or "recite." They had, however, shot some bullets into the socially prominent millionaire, W. E. D. Stokes, and while the newspapers were still carrying four-inch headlines about the case, Willie grabbed the ladies and billed them as "The Shooting Stars." They were the worst act in the history of the theatre, but they packed the house, acquired an agent and demanded more money for an extended engagement. Willie agreed on one condition—that they go out and shoot another millionaire.

Looking around for another dame prepared adequately and properly to defend her honor, Willie next found Florence Carman, who shot one of her doctor-husband's lady patients. Before the bullet had been dug out of the patient, Willie had Florence signed up. Florence, however, had other talents. She could sing. It was Florence who gave the world of music its tenderest rendition of the song "Baby Shoes."

After a week's engagement at the Victoria, another of Willie's murderous celebrities hired Harry Reichenbach as her agent to see that she remained prominent in the public eye. The dauntless Reichenbach proceeded to find luxurious quarters for her in Juárez, Mexico, and, to account for her presence there, spread the story that her beloved brother, a wealthy oil magnate, had been kidnaped by Mexican bandits and she was trying to find him. Reichenbach then arranged an interview for her with Pancho

Villa to discuss her brother's plight. He left her with strict instructions to stagger from Villa's chambers after a suitable time with clothes awry and bleeding from a few self-inflicted pen-knife nicks. He would take it from there. Hour followed hour and the lady failed to emerge. She was not seen until the following night, when she emerged on Villa's arm, rosy, smiling and bound for dinner and an evening of gaiety. This unexpected turn, Reichenbach said, "certainly cut off her career with Hammerstein but it probably opened up new vistas for her with Villa."

After Harry Thaw killed Stanford White on the old Madison Square Garden roof garden over Evelyn Nesbitt Thaw, Willie, naturally, had Evelyn hog-tied to a contract within an hour. It would have been sooner but Evelyn held out on the billing. Willie's idea of billing was "Mrs. Thaw." Evelyn's was "Miss Nesbitt." Miss Nesbitt won, but she did not reach her peak in audience popularity until later, when Thaw escaped from Matteawan, where he had been committed for insanity. Following this escape, Willie let it be known from all rooftops that Evelyn "feared for her life" and convinced the Police Department that she should be assigned a uniformed police squad to escort her day and night, particularly into and out of (and with suitable photography) the Victoria. As *Show Biz* has recalled, Willie was uncharitably accused by envious rivals of having actually engineered Thaw's "coincidental escape."

Willie died in 1914, the most mourned and the most loved showman on Broadway, and I should add, in due credit, that Willie introduced more real, legitimate talent to Broadway than his successor, the Palace, ever did. The

Victoria was taken over by his brother, Arthur, who loathed
sensationalism, and one of his first riddances was a sketch
which Willie had booked called "Electrocution." In it,
an actor-prisoner sat strapped in an electric chair and a list
of his offenses against society was intoned. The list was
formidable and interminable. It included, as I remember,
grand larceny, kidnaping, rape, murder (I might be getting
him confused here with some of my Rialto heroes), dope-
addiction, mopery, mother-beating and several other
charges which I have forgotten—he had had an incredibly
busy and mischievous career. The climax of this idyl came
when the actor-warden could not force himself to pull the
switch because he "did not believe in capital punishment,"
whereupon volunteers from the audience were invited to
come up on the stage and pull the switch. When there
were volunteers—and there were many—the doomed man
would slump in his chair realistically as fake sparks went
off just back of it.

Two years after Willie's death the Victoria died. It was
reborn the Rialto, a motion picture theatre, under the
direction of Roxy. Roxy rebuilt it in opulent—or Roxy—
style and reopened it on April 21, 1916, "with the peal of
the grand organ and to the fanfare of iridescent lights,"
according to an old press release written by Roxy himself.
Another Roxy-written release modestly identified it as
"Temple of Motion Pictures, Shrine of Music and the
Allied Arts." The New York *American* called it "a veritable
triumph—staggering in its splendor." Roxy staged ballets,
put elegant uniforms on the ushers and gave them pearled
and luminous batons to carry in directing customers to

their seats. He hired Hugo Riesenfeld to conduct the thirty-five piece orchestra and crowned him "Doctor" Riesenfeld, an honorary degree which backfired on him the very first week after the coronation when a customer was stricken in the middle of the Moonlight Sonata and demanded that she be attended by the pit doctor.

Owing to Roxy's pre-eminence in the show world, and also to his solid financial backing—one of his backers was the owner of the magazine *The American Golfer*, which explains an incongruous advertising trailer which interrupted proceedings on the screen every half hour no matter how suspenseful or tender the moment—Roxy was usually able to get the best in pictures. Even he, however, had occasional trouble with the highjack practices of the producers and distributors. His talented press agent, none other than Terry Ramsaye, who also helped the owners keep an eye on Roxy's well-known prodigality with other people's money, found the answer to this problem. He wrote reviews of forthcoming pictures and gave them to the newspapers, whose representatives in those days greatly appreciated having their work done for them. Most of Ramsaye's reviews were favorable, even on occasions when the pictures were only passable, but when the film rental was still in dispute he would pan them mercilessly. Several distributors were guided in this manner to see the light.

In time, Roxy moved on and Riesenfeld took over. Under his aegis, *Heliotrope*, a Hearst-owned film, created first-night history of sorts. The particular audience which showed up that night stole everything that wasn't nailed down—even the cuspidors. It was never discovered why

Mr. Hearst's *Heliotrope* should have attracted so many kleptomaniacs.

In the early twenties Zukor brought the theatre under the Paramount banner. During the ensuing years it maintained its position as one of the country's leading theatres by playing such films as *Kid Boots*, *Shanghai Express*, *The Patriot*, *Dishonored*, *The Trespasser* and *The Way of All Flesh*. Under Publix management, however, the better pictures were moved into the Paramount Theatre. Rialto receipts, along with its prestige, promptly fell apart. It was at this juncture that the regimented regime vacated and the ramshackle Mayer management took over.

· XI ·

DURING THE YEARS that the Rialto and I were partners in crime, I was concurrently engaged in a number of outside activities. I became the trustee for a bankrupt hotel, the owner of a farm fully equipped with hungry chickens, a second-hand tractor and an orchard requiring seven sprayings a year. In a frenetic moment, I invested some money in a new kind of parachute for amusement park jumping (guaranteed not to break more than one neck out of ten). Word of this venture got around and I was shortly known up and down Broadway as an easy mark for inventions, the freakier the better. For quite a period thereafter, my office was a mecca for peculiar-looking individuals, most of whom resembled a cross between Slapsey Maxie Rosenbloom and one of Jehovah's Witnesses. Unable to resist consistently their blandishments, I invested in a novel type

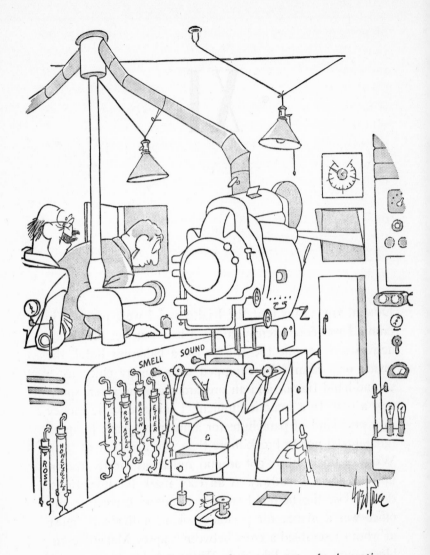

I was known up and down Broadway as a patsy for inventions.

of permanent wave machine but nothing came of it because the inventor promptly and permanently disappeared from town. I dallied with popcorn guaranteed to provide silent theatre mastication, but it proved tasteless as well as crunchless. I was let in on the ground floor of a combination flashlight and pencil, which seemed a fine idea to me until I found that the same gadget had been on the market for a year under other auspices and other patronage, but under the same patent as the one offered me.

One day, however, a quite sane and honorable visitor brought in a device which he modestly proclaimed to be the greatest advance in movie technique since the advent of the talkies. It was an odor track attached to a film—much like a sound track—and as it passed through the projection machine, it propelled into the auditorium exactly the right smell at exactly the right moment. He had prepared a sample film which he demonstrated. The first scene was located in an autumnal apple orchard, where two young lovers had built a fire and were cooking their lunch. The propelled odors were burning leaves, fallen (and exceedingly ripe) apples and bacon. The next sequence was in a church, where the couple was being married in front of an altar of roses and honeysuckle. The last scene was in a hospital corridor where—a natural sequence in love stories—the new father was getting the happy news that it was a boy, amid reeking fumes of ether and disinfectant.

The blowers which wafted these odors out with such precision were supposed to waft them back with equal efficiency, but unfortunately this part of the invention had not yet been entirely perfected. The auditorium was so full of a mingling of honeysuckle, bacon and lysol that it took over an hour to clear the air and for several days afterward there was such a strong smell of those mature apples around that a friend asked me if I was making applejack on the side. It was a long time before I finally lost confidence in the smellies, but my man and I—I had become a zealous partisan if not a partner—could never seem to master the backward waft.

To achieve bankruptcy with the least delay, however, I recommend the legitimate theatre, particularly if you are unlucky enough to pick a winner the first time out, as I did. The play was *The Old Maid*, which starred Judith Anderson and Helen Menken and which won the year's Pulitzer Prize for 1934-35, a selection, incidentally, which aroused so much unfavorable comment that The New York Drama Critics Circle was established to make its own Annual Awards.

The Old Maid was produced by an old friend of mine, Harry Moses, who, when I first met him, was a highly esteemed Chicago underwear manufacturer. His transformation into a theatrical magnate was solely due to his hyperthyroid spouse, Elsa, who was what we used to call "stagestruck." As a consequence, Harry was soon stuck with a small professional theatrical group in which she was a major participant. This was at a time when Stanislavsky and the Moscow Art Theatre were regarded by chichi circles west of the Hudson as the last word in stage technique.

Naturally, the plays had to have a Russian director, and

naturally, more and more money was required to keep the company afloat. Harry, torn between the lofty requirements of art and the elementary principles of business, awoke to find himself one day a substantial investor in a close-to-defunct theatrical enterprise. He wished to continue to contribute to his wife's happiness but not to contribute on a scale calculated to impoverish him. So he called upon the maestro for something in the nature of collateral. Nothing was available except the script of a new play. The devotees of Stanislavsky, who worked more by ear and instinct than by the written word, regarded all scripts disparagingly, but any security is better than none, and Harry took it. When eventually the group collapsed, he and Elsa reread the script and decided that it was a lot better than many plays they had seen. This favorable opinion, however, was not shared by the New York producing fraternity to whom he offered it, with the exception of the astute Mr. Herman Shumlin, who waxed enthusiastic. Shumlin, then in the early stages of his distinguished career, agreed to direct and to act as coproducer with Moses. *Grand Hotel* established Shumlin's reputation as a fine director and made more money for Harry Moses during its long New York run and through its sale to the movies than he had saved in an entire lifetime of hard work and careful application to the highest principles of the underwear business.

His next success was *The Old Maid*, to which my only contributions were financial. This was not due to any self-effacement on my part. As an experienced movie man, I was convinced that I was a gift from heaven to the legitimate branch of the industry, and attempted to live up to this exalted role at every conceivable opportunity. My suggestions, it must be admitted, were not gratefully welcomed. Indeed, after receiving for a few weeks my daily barrage of constructive comments, our eminent director issued orders that whenever I was seen entering the Empire Theatre, where rehearsals were being held, the curtain was automatically to be dropped.

In spite, or possibly because, of this failure to appreciate my talents, *The Old Maid* proved a box-office bonanza as well as an artistic triumph. We sold it for forty thousand dollars, a substantial sum in those days, to Paramount. Once they had purchased it they became, in accordance with an old Hollywood custom, convinced that it required substantial revisions before it would be suitable for the screen. Over a period of years they exhausted a bevy of screen writers in a vain effort to improve on Edith Wharton, who had written the original story. Eventually, in discouragement, they sold the rights to Warner Brothers, who promptly produced a picture closely adhering to the stage version. With Bette Davis and Miriam Hopkins in the leading roles, it fully satisfied the demands of the Hays organization as well as the taste of the public, and proved a great success. There is an ancient wheeze that Hollywood buys a good story about a bad girl and makes it into a bad story about a good girl. No such indignity was committed on *The Old Maid.*

In the meantime, Harry and myself as well as our stagewise legal confrere, Irving Ottenberg, had invested all of our profits in *Oh Evening Star,* another play by Zoe Akins, the adapter of *The Old Maid*. The "star" shone dimly over Broadway for less than a week.

As a consequence of this and a few subsequent disasters, I reached the conclusion that the Broadway drama was too rich a gambling diet even for my voracious appetite. Consequently, when my friend Oscar Serlin one day offered me a ten-thousand-dollar interest in a new show he was promoting, I omnisciently assured him that it had "very slim box-office appeal." It was *Life with Father*, which still holds the record for Broadway's longest run.

With singed wings, I transferred my angeling activities to my own back yard, where, as soon as I had regained my old self-confidence, not to mention a new bankroll, I began to invest in pictures, among them a series known as *The East Side Kids*, concerned with the adventures of some nauseating adolescents. They were adolescents, that is, when the series started. But the series met with so much success and so many of these pictures were made that long before it was finished they were grown men and even less attractive. Archer Winsten, the usually kindly movie critic of the New York *Post*, wrote of one of these pictures, "Connoisseurs of the worst in movie-making cannot afford to pass up this triple-distilled exudate from the pores of a long dead movie carcass." The picture referred to was one of the best of the lot—not one of which failed to return a profit of over one hundred per cent.

Many years later, during World War II, I was the guest one night of an admiral in the New Hebrides. After dinner, as a special treat for me, he took me to see a movie which he had already seen, but which he had enjoyed so much that he would be glad, he said, to sit through it again. Settled in our seats, what should I see romp onto the screen but *The East Side Kids*, where they disported themselves to the delight of several hundred sailors in the audience. The picture was the same one that Winsten had so adequately characterized.

As a result of the success of *The East Side Kids* pictures, their producer, Sam Katzman, was promoted to a high-salaried job with Columbia Pictures. One day I screened a fine film, at least fine by Rialto standards, with numerous sanguinary murders and no emphasis on the true and the beautiful. A hard-hearted salesman, however, said that I could not play it unless I also contracted for another Columbia gem, Sam Katzman's *Last of the Mohicans*. Such was the practice of distributors before block-booking was legally abolished. So I looked at the Katzman epic. To raise the price to the exhibitors, it had been made in color of some early vintage inspired by a lover of chromos. The faces of the performers were patches of crimson and green. The foliage was blue and strange streaks of orange and crimson vibrated occasionally across the passionate purple sky. The Mohicans were fresh out of Harlem and their canoes prominently displayed the Abercrombie & Fitch label. I protested to my old pal, Abe Montague, chief of Columbia's distribution, that although Rialto audiences were of a notably receptive and uncritical character, there was a limit even to their readiness to accept anything offered to them. All to no avail. Abe was adamant. Eventually I played the two pictures. The one I liked was, at best, mildly successful. My patrons adored *Last of the Mohicans*.

To demonstrate that I was now a well-established character in the theatrical world, I invariably lunched every mid-day at the same table at Sardi's. The table next to me was, with equal certainty, occupied by Jake Wilk, then the sagacious book and play reader for Warner Brothers. Jake was largely responsible for the momentous period in which that company selected for production one magnificent social document after another, from *The Life of Emile Zola* in 1937 through *Watch on the Rhine* in 1943. Incidentally and sadly, it might be added, few of these fine adult films proved to be box-office successes.

Mr. Wilk, as befits a man whose superb selections were so little appreciated, is invariably morose. One day he was, if possible, more gloomy than ever. Over his canneloni he confided to me that his organization had decided that it was no longer profitable, or even regarded as praiseworthy, to make propaganda films. Consequently, they were passing up a new book entitled *Education for Death*, which he was confident, if translated into picture terms, would awaken the American public to the world menace of the Nazi plan of militarism and totalitarianism. Possibly, however, the brothers Warner were in a measure motivated by a lack of faith in the book's commercial values, for only a few weeks subsequently they undertook the production of *Mission to Moscow*, which was later, under the proddings of the Un-American Activities Committee, to occasion them considerable embarrassment.

Jake expatiated so eloquently on the educational values inherent in *Education for Death* that in a moment of public spirit I not only offered to obtain a producer but even to make a small investment in so worthy a project. I suggested as the ideal man to take over the enterprise Mr. Edward Golden. Golden is affectionately known throughout the picture industry as "Doc," partially as a tribute to the diploma he claims to hold from Tufts Medical College, primarily because of the resuscitory services he has rendered to numerous independent productions. "Doc" has one endearing weakness: he frequently distributes an interest in his productions to so many of his good friends that it is not unusual for him to awake some morning to discover that he has given away one hundred and ten per cent of the project, leaving nothing except glory for Golden. His unorthodox, though innocent, methods are reminiscent of those used by another distinguished artist in another field, Max Baer, who, after he had managed to sell a few hundred per cent of himself, was disconcerted to discover that business transactions, unlike baseball averages, are not figured on a one thousand per cent formula.

Only a short time previous to the period of which I am speaking, Golden had completed a picture entitled *No Greater Sin*, dealing with the delicate subject of syphilis so discreetly that it met with the approval both of the Catholic hierarchy and of exhibitors mindful of the box-office potentialities of so tantalizing a topic. Few others have been skillful enough to navigate with such success between the Scylla of propriety and the Charybdis of commerce.

We entrusted *Education for Death* to Golden's skillful hands and had no excuse for our surprise at a later date

196

when it emerged as a box-office chiller entitled *Hitler's Children*. This title, later justly regarded as one of the reasons for the film's amazing success (it was probably the most sensational "sleeper," or unexpected box-office hit, in movie annals), was originally rejected by RKO, to whom we turned for its distribution.

Golden, who had a greater flair for titles and talent than for finance, employed a comparatively unknown author, Emmett Lavery, to write the screenplay, and an equally unrecognized director, Eddie Dmytryk, to handle the megaphone. The picture made the reputations of both men. It led to fame and popularity for Lavery and eventually to a convict's cell for Dmytryk, who was one of the Hollywood Ten who refused to answer the Un-American Activities Committee's inquiry as to whether or not they were Communists.

We merchandised *Hitler's Children* with one of the first picture campaigns conducted largely on national radio networks. This was a startling innovation as at that time radio was regarded as a sinister threat to the future of the movies, which, ostrichlike, they should ignore rather than conciliate. A similar obtuse attitude toward television presently prevails in some high-echelon picture circles. Our lobby displays consisted of lurid paper showing handsome young women with well-exposed torsos being flogged for their refusal to cohabit with Nazi supermen, and our newspaper advertising hinted at even more drastic and indelicate forms of punishment for those who prized their virtue more than the production of cannon fodder for the Fatherland. The total cash investment made by myself and a few other quasi-capitalists amounted to $20,000. The balance of the incredibly low production budget of $160,000 was promoted from distributors and the laboratory. The net profit to the entrepreneurs approximated $2,000,000. Rarely has devotion to the common weal been rewarded so generously and so promptly this side of heaven.

Encouraged by such profitable errors of judgment, I purchased, in conjunction with two enterprising and able exhibitors, Artie Rapf and Mike Ruden, a theatre in Somerville, New Jersey, or to be more accurate, two theatres, one of which in accordance with the first principles of theatre operation we promptly converted into a garage so as to establish a "closed situation." This forestalled any local competition and enabled us to pay the film exchanges what we regarded as reasonable rentals—a conclusion with which the picture distributors rarely agreed.

At this juncture I had been naïvely impressed by questionnaires, circulated by public opinion research agencies, demonstrating the unfavorable reaction of movie patrons to double features. Invariably the answers indicated a sentiment of more than two to one against two pictures for the price of one. I prevailed upon my reluctant partners, smarter men than I, to experiment with a policy of one outstanding feature on the week-ends. The good burghers of Somerville, however, as well as their spouses and offspring, refused to be deprived of their entertainment bargain. On Saturdays and Sundays they drove to the nearby town of Bound Brook, where my friend and canny competitor, George Skouras, reaped a rich, unearned harvest until we reverted to sanity and a second feature. At the

present time, in some of the, theatrically speaking, de-
pressed areas, double features have not only been replaced
by triple features but actually by quadruplays, or whatever
worse name you can devise for four pictures.

I also helped to promote and build the Washington
Trans-Lux Theatre and acquired an interest in other houses
of the Trans-Lux circuit. At that time this consisted of a
group of prosperous and commodious little newsreel theatres. Its chief stockholder, a grand old goateed English
gentleman, Percy Furber, had been a mining engineer in
Mexico and regarded all American presidents since William McKinley as wild and reprehensible radicals. In small
and meticulous handwriting he had kept notebooks for over
forty years with complete details of his exemplary daily activities. This is a practice which I heartily recommend to
sufficiently industrious neophytes, for these records saved
our hides a few years later when we were sued by a real
estate broker whose memory for dates was fortunately as
unreliable as his allegations. I, on the other hand, almost
caused a mistrial. On the final day of legal summations, in
my ignorance of correct court procedures, I distributed theatre passes to the attendants as an indication of my appreciation of their courtesies during the two weeks of the trial.
The realtor's attorney, incensed at such largesse, arose and
denounced me in most distressing terms. A show-wise judge,
however, after ascertaining that the passes were not for
Oklahoma! but only for the Rialto, ruled that they constituted no bribe.

The operation of newsreel theatres was, until recently,
the nearest approach to the ideal of making a living with

a minimum of effort ever devised by human ingenuity. At the beginning of each season you contracted for all five newsreels and then sat down and prayed for earthquakes, floods, plane crashes and elopements of millionaire debutantes with their chauffeurs. The worse the news, the better your business—and there was plenty of bad news.

These idyllic conditions were too perfect to endure permanently. Television's capacity to bring unpleasant tidings directly and daily into the home has greatly curtailed the popularity of newsreels and brought to an untimely end the ample leisure, not to mention the ample profits, of newsreel theatre operation.

With all of my mongrel interests, I could not continue to spend twenty-four hours a day at the Rialto as I had originally done. I began to stay away a few hours a day, then half days, then whole days. Without me business continued as usual. When I was absent for several consecutive days, receipts improved surprisingly. When I stayed away once for two weeks in a row, grosses soared to the highest mark ever achieved under my management. I ascribed this to the picture, to the weather, to the season of the year and to that old stand-by, "It's just in the air, that's all." When one of my outside activities took me out of the country and I did not see Forty-second Street and Broadway for many, many months, five new box-office records were made and several unprecedented four-week runs ensued. I found it puzzling, but no one else on the staff seemed to share my surprise.

This latter activity was World War II. I was a Treasury dollar-a-year man (when I was paid off with a one-cent check by Henry Morgenthau, Jr., I cashed it); I was one of the executives of the War Activities Committee of the Motion Picture Industry (referred to as the WAC for the sake of brevity and the utmost confusion); I was Film Consultant to the Secretary of War, and as Special Representative of the Chairman of the American Red Cross I traveled all over the world.

In these many and various jobs I had many and various duties. Among them was to see that the industry's films, given gratis for showing to the Armed Forces, were distributed in every theatre of war. I was, consequently, on planes that dropped films by parachute to men deep in the jungles and on pack mules that carried them high up in the Apennines. I helped to get them shown on decks of transports and hospital ships, in theatres dug out of hillsides, in ice-encrusted Nissen huts, in caves, and in bombed-out monasteries. At Guadalcanal we screened movies in a tent twenty-four hours a day, to men fresh from front-line service and too emotionally exhausted to sleep. We showed pictures, in fact, wherever and whenever it was humanly possible to do so, and in no other endeavor have I ever felt such a challenge, or made such an effort to meet it, or felt less adequate.

Ordinarily a picture was shown for three days and then forwarded to the next stop, but if the new, incoming film was held up or lost in transit, the current show was held over. The same audience saw it again. And again. On arriving in the Marianas once, the commanding officer and two Red Cross girls told me they had watched *Going My Way* for seven successive nights and they were all beginning to loathe not only the Barry Fitzgerald brogue but all Ireland. In that same audience one night, eleven Japs were captured who had sneaked in to see the picture. It was suggested that they be permitted to see the end of the picture before being sent to the compound, but they declined with profuse but meaningful thanks. They, too, had seen it for several nights in a row, they confessed—with a slight brogue.

World premières were held all over the world and were called "foxhole premières." I saw *Saratoga Trunk* in France and *Mark Twain* on shipboard in the Pacific more than a year before their general release. *Wilson* had its first showing in Okinawa only a few miles behind the front. The show lasted four and a half hours because it was interrupted three times by air raids. I saw *The Fighting Lady* first in Hawaii. A super Steichen-supervised Technicolor story of adventure aboard an aircraft carrier, *The Fighting Lady* knew she had been in a fight when she got through with that first-night audience. It was composed of convalescing submarine sailors who greeted scenes of flat-top life with boos, ribaldry, catcalls and Bronx cheers. When the show was over most of them said they had enjoyed it more than any picture they had ever seen. They certainly were the noisiest audience I had ever encountered.

I also helped to make and distribute all types of war shorts. They were devised to encourage, among innumerable other things, food saving, field morale, home morality, recruiting and combat training. In regard to the last, I once saw a group of fresh recruits sit through a training film which showed in graphic detail how to gouge eyes, kick groins and effect other impressive though even more grisly mayhem, all of which demonstrated that good sportsmanship is a sentiment in which no soldier in a tight spot could afford to indulge. It was so grim and tough I had feared it would be too disconcerting for young Americans. The boys took it without a quiver, but two of their number fainted dead away at the following film on the program, which dealt with the consequences of venereal disease.

In Burma, a serious danger was the prevalence of malarial mosquitoes. To instruct the natives in a few elementary precautions, we made some film slides greatly magnifying the size of the mosquito so as to illustrate clearly the means by which the deadly parasite is transmitted. At the first showing of these slides the audience, to my dismay, burst into peals of laughter. I asked a Chinese Red Cross boy seated next to me the cause of the merriment. "In America," he said, "you have big mosquitoes and they must be, as you say, a big danger. But here we have very, very little ones which give you very, very little itch. Elephant mosquitoes are very, very funny."

Most of the Army films were produced in the old Paramount studios at Astoria, New York, which had been idle since 1935. The previous occupants, Ben Hecht and Charlie MacArthur, had operated it as no studio has ever been conducted before or since. Above the desks in their office hung pictures of nude gals in seductive poses, calculated to distract the attention of worried sales executives solicitous to know when they would get their next picture, and of even more worried bankers solicitous to know when they would get their money back. The delays in production were not entirely inexplicable as the eminent producers preferred a few laughs a day to a few feet of finished film, and there was much goosing of cameramen, showgirls and dignified visitors. On the walls, if I remember correctly, there were signs reading, "If it's good enough for Zukor it isn't good enough for us," and "We are going to make a picture a year if it takes us four years." In spite of the atmosphere of rowdy good-fellowship, maybe because of it, they turned out far better pictures—*Crime Without Passion* and *The Scoundrel*, for instance—than more businesslike gentry.

The Army instituted an even more incredible regime at Astoria. Corpulent Hollywood executives clad in Fifth Avenue-tailored GI uniforms drove to reveille every morning in Cadillacs and Chryslers—the only motorized Signal Corps in military annals. They ate lunch reluctantly at the Army mess but dined nightly at New York's most expensive and exclusive restaurants. They were billeted at an Eighth Avenue hotel but most of them lived sumptuously at the Waldorf or the Plaza. And their military talk was interspersed with chatter of past and future productions and big money transactions; in fact, other envious branches of the service referred to them as the "greenback recruits."

Among them was Arnaud D'Usseau, the playright and scenarist (*Scarface* was one of his successes), who was on KP duty one day when a telephone message came through from his able and alert agent, Leah Salisbury. A hard-hearted sergeant answered the call and refused to let her talk to her high-priced property because he was busy peeling potatoes. The sergeant instructed her to give him any messages she had for his man. When he was through relaying the conversation back and forth his eyes and ears were bugged out like bubble gum. "The dame says you can get seventy-five thousand dollars," was his first relay. The final one from Arnaud, or so it was reported as he removed an eye from a spud, was, "Tell her it's one hundred thousand on the line or the deal is cold."

Another of my favorite Astoria stories, probably equally apocryphal, tells of one of its units which moved into General Brehon Somervell's office one day to shoot a brief sequence in which the General appeared. He appeared, but there was a touch of apoplexy about his movie debut, and for an understandable reason. A lowly and most un-military-appearing Pfc was apparently in command of the situation. He instructed his sergeant on how to handle the lights, relegated to his lieutenant the menial task of carrying the equipment, and with no unnecessary formalities told the General what to do and what not to do. The Pfc was George Cukor, the celebrated director of *David Copperfield*, *Little Women* and many other splendid productions.

In spite of their peculiarities, maybe because of them, the Hollywood alumni assembled at Astoria did a memorable job. Under Colonel Emanuel Cohen, a former editor of the *Paramount News* as well as chief executive of its studio—so small a man that Jack Oakie, after talking to him, always went around limping with a pretended crick in his back—the shooting stages and cutting rooms were transformed into beehives turning out films on every imaginable subject from How to Wash to Elements of Electricity. The latter utilized animation and diagrams to demonstrate the interrelation of neutrons and protons, and to explain what an atom really is. I saw it five times and still don't know, but that was my fault and not the film's.

Thirty-six GI's with only three weeks of Army training —none of it in engineering work—were shown a Signal Corps training film entitled *How to Build a Timber Trestle Bridge*. They screened the movie only once. Then they were taken out in the country with a sergeant equally inexperienced and told to build a bridge. According to an Engineering Major, "In three and a half hours they had completed a forty-five-foot timber trestle bridge as good as any I have ever seen. If that isn't an argument for training films, I'll eat one!"

Some Army officers estimated that the use of these teaching films—popularly known as "nuts and bolts"—cut the training period by as much as forty per cent. Although this estimate seems to me unduly optimistic, there can be no doubt that they demonstrated once and for all the merits of visual education.

Whenever I could get a day off and wherever I happened to be in my travels, I always took a busman's holiday and tried to find some kind of movie activity. Once I visited a studio on the outskirts of Calcutta at Tollygunge, generally referred to as Tollywood. Technically it was on a par with the first studio I ever saw at Fort Lee, New Jersey, in the early twenties. A de luxe thirty-thousand-dollar production—the price of an American short—was being shot. The one camera was dollied back and forth by three turbaned, skinny stage-hands; a small boy circulated with drinking water, and there were—but no more than in Hollywood—inexplicable delays, endless retakes and interminable conferences. The actors read their lines adequately but listlessly, the heat was intense, and I was beginning to nod, myself, when the studio manager started to dart around whispering something to everyone. Following this, the studio suddenly became as animated as an old Mack Sennett cop chase. The male lead viriled up, turned into a lens louse and tried to steal every scene. The ingénue began to emote like an Eddie Cantor playing an orphans' home benefit, the director stormed and struck poses, the cameramen began to do ballets with the camera, and the villain began to frighten even me. I wondered what magic words the studio manager had whispered to effect this transformation. I did not have to wonder long because shortly he himself came over to me with an interpreter in tow who bowed low and said, "It is an honor to have in our midst so outstanding a representative of Western culture as the celebrated Mr. Louis B. Mayer, maestro of so cultured an organization as the M-G-M Corporation of America." After trying in vain for twenty minutes to correct this misunderstanding, I sneaked out, leaving in my wake, I am afraid, several dashed hopes for Hollywood contracts.

On a subsequent occasion, when in Rome, I had a private audience with Pope Pius XII. It was one of the great hours of my life. I found His Holiness a man of rare warmth, charm and erudition. The primary purpose of the audience was to discuss the relief operations of the Red Cross, but we were soon talking about motion pictures, with which he seemed well acquainted. He had not, however, yet seen the Italian film *Open City*, which I had just screened and which had excited me hugely. He had had a report about it and, in striking contrast with the subsequent attitude of American Catholic prelates, found no fault with the memorable scene in which a priest, seeking to shield an anti-Nazi, deceives the agents of the Gestapo by pretending to extend the Last Sacrament to a dying man. He told me, however, that many American films seemed injurious to the preservation of high moral standards and the sanctity of the marriage bond. We must have talked for over an hour and after I left I was fearful that in His Holiness' friendly and kindly aura I had become perhaps too loquacious and argumentative.

It was with a mixture of relief and envy that I heard later that His Holiness had reported to our Envoy to the Vatican that he had greatly enjoyed "the visit with your Mr. Louis B. Mayer."

On other days off I visited the theatres and studios in Germany, China, Japan and Israel. I was impressed with a charming custom in one Chungking picture house. When a tragedy was played there, warm, damp face towels were distributed to the more sensitive patrons on which to wipe their tear-stained faces. I was also fascinated by the "speakers" known as "benshi" in Japanese theatres. Instead of long, explanatory captions on foreign films—chiefly American—these commentators would describe the action on the screen with lines such as, "Now the husband enters the room. What does he see? Oh, horror of horrors, his bride is in the arms of his best friend. His wrath is overwhelming. He strikes his best friend to the floor with his fists. He wins! But, alas, all is lost." Many of these "benshi" attained great popularity; in fact, frequently their names were more prominently featured on the marquees than the titles of the pictures or the American stars who appeared in them. It was the billing no doubt that impressed me. As a veteran sufferer at the hands of billing-crazy American stars, it was not an altogether unpleasant sight to me to see one, Tomio Mori, take a four-inch precedence over a certain actress who had once torn my hair out for three inches less.

In Shanghai I became an actor myself for a brief and inadvertent moment. I had checked into the Pacific Hotel so tired, battered and bedraggled that I felt like the sparrow who got mixed up in the badminton game. I was undressing for the first time in days and interested in nothing in the world but a bath and bed, when the Chinese equivalent of a house dick knocked on the door. China being at the opposite side of the world from the United States, its morals and manners are frequently the complete reverse of ours. The dick did not look under the bed but asked in his best pidgin English, "Want gur?"

"Want what?" I asked.

"Gur," answered the hospitable hotel representative. He then proceeded with appropriate gestures to indicate clearly what a "gur" was and what a "gur" could do. His pantomime was so perfect that I had little trouble grasping the idea. I wearily pointed to my gray hair and to my eyeglasses as a reasonable excuse for my strange lack of interest in the suggestion. As a pantomime artist, however, I appar-

ently laid an egg. Half an hour later there was again a
knock on my door. The dick had returned wreathed in
smiles. There was no accounting for the tastes of these
amazing Americans, but he was the man to satisfy even
the most unreasonable. He was accompanied by a charming if somewhat mature Russian lady, her blonde hair
streaked with gray, and wearing pince-nez.

Operating behind the scenes of theatres, clubs, canteens,
hospitals and all other gathering places, I occasionally felt
momentarily useful, but many, many times, with nothing
to offer the soldiers by way of relaxation or entertainment,
I had to fall back on my own conversational resources.
These were indeed lame and ignoble. My opening gambit
was always, "Where do you come from?" Frequently,
thanks to Publix, I could recall the boy's local movie house
and talk about it, the pictures it played, and occasionally
I was lucky enough to have known the manager.

In other cases, to establish a channel of communication
and confidence I had to resort to some liberal ad-libbing.
I talked about movie stars and claimed, heaven forgive me,
to have known all of them intimately. Having never hoisted
even a glass of milk with either, I told of drinking bouts
with W. C. Fields and John Barrymore. I told of gay (and
intime) evenings with Lana, Gloria, Jennifer and Rita; I
described what they wore and what they said, and gave
fan magazine descriptions of their homes and swimming
pools. I gossiped about several fanciful romances including
one which had a reasonably accurate basis. I told of how
Vivien Leigh traveled six thousand miles to Hollywood
just to be near the man she loved, Laurence Olivier, who

was making the picture *Rebecca*, how she could not marry
him at the time, and how, as a consequence of this love,
she came to David Selznick's attention and was selected
for the part of Scarlett O'Hara. The moral of the story,
and one that every homesick boy in uniform relished, was
that love triumphs. I went too far with Vivien—all the way
to Atlanta, Georgia, in fact, for the world première of
Gone With the Wind—a trip which proved a mistake. I
told how the band met her (and me) at the railroad station playing "Dixie" and that I heard her say, "How sweet
of them, they're playing the theme song from our picture."
I got my laugh, but unfortunately one of the boys was
from Atlanta and although a youngster at the time, clearly
remembered, or claimed to remember, every detail of the
première. He was certain that Vivien had not been there.
He also pointed out that he had heard the story pinned
on Olivia de Havilland and he continued to ask me further
test questions about that opening. The questions became
too testy for me and I broke down and confessed to all.
(I found out later that Vivien did attend the opening.)

I hope as a listener all over the world I made up for
what I lacked as a talker. Certainly there was more sincerity
in it. In Europe men just rescued from German prison
camps brought lumps to my throat when they asked such
questions as: "When I get home do you think my wife will
think I've changed too much for her still to love me?"
And showing me an old photograph, one said proudly,
"See. This is what I used to look like." Some had kept
diaries which they read to me—frequently laden with
entries as to what they would like to eat when they got

home. Almost all had pictures of their families worn thin by loving handling, which they would show to any sympathetic visitor. Once in Nice, where the most luxurious casino on the Riviera had been converted into a recreation center, a tall, lanky boy from Iowa looked at the richly upholstered floor and said, "Is that a real carpet, sir?" I assured him it was and he took off his shoes and socks and walked on it "just to get the feel again of a carpet." He then tenderly recalled to me the carpet in his mother's parlor at home, the color, the size of the roses in it, the price and the details of the day it was put down. It was to him "much prettier than this rug here."

In an Army hospital in Naples, a convalescent boy was painting murals on the bare walls of the reception hall. He was not painting what he had seen and suffered on the frozen Rapido River, nor was he painting the blue of the Bay of Naples or any scenes of Vesuvius. He was working on two pictures: one of a piney slope with a small house in the foreground surrounded by a picket fence—his own home in Missouri; and the other, a baseball park with a couple of players on base wearing red-trimmed uniforms with the name "Cardinals" painted on their blouses. Another Cardinal was at bat. He was trying to re-create what, in spite of his war experiences, still seemed to him the greatest moment he had ever lived through.

Before the murals were completed the Colonel in command of the hospital called the painter into his office and said, "I have wonderful news for you. You're going home."

"That's good," the boy said. "How soon?"

"Day after tomorrow."

To the Colonel's amazement the boy stammered and turned pale. "But I can't go then," he said, "my pictures aren't finished."

When the big transport pushed off with its decks jammed with whistling, gleeful boys, he was not even on the pier to wave good-by. He was on the scaffold with his beloved home team.

In these few scattered recollections of my travels I hope I have not given the impression that the war was, to me, a lark. I have purposefully omitted my most poignant memories and impressions (and the mention of many people who were dear to me) because they are of a kind that I lack the talent to write about, nor do I have—and for many reasons—the inclination. When the war ended I hung up my uniform and returned to Forty-second Street and Broadway. But only for a brief interval. The War Department asked me to return to Europe as Chief of the Motion Picture Branch of Military Government in Germany. We were, or so I was told, to re-create the German film industry along modern, progressive lines and help, through the production and circulation of documentaries, "to inculcate democratic ideas, the respect for human rights and the development of individual political responsibility." This seemed too challenging a program to miss, so, although movie business was booming, I made the supreme sacrifice and, to make myself completely available, sold the Rialto. My subsequent services in Germany did little to advance the cause of democratic institutions, but it should be reported that I disposed of my theatre interests at the most favorable moment, and that never before or since has the lease of a movie theatre of similar size been sold for a comparable sum. Virtue may, as reported, be its own reward—but I have always found it highly remunerative.

· XII ·

BACK IN my early Rialto days I developed another activity
which proved lots of fun and occasionally profitable. Oscar
Serlin, who had unavailingly sought to make me wealthy
with an interest in *Life With Father,* but who was then still
a lynx-eyed Paramount talent scout, had unearthed a Russian cartoon type of feature made with puppets, called *The
New Gulliver.* Apparently the boys in the back room at
Moscow regarded its good-natured spoofing of the prole-
tariat as "deviationist" and "counterrevolutionary" and had
vetoed its distribution by Amkino, their film representatives
in the United States. On the other hand, my connection
with *Gulliver* was resurrected against me years later when
I was appointed Film Consultant to the E.C.A. In the
F.B.I's judgment, a man who had distributed a Russian
film in 1935, even one frowned on by the Politburo, might

well be a subversive character. Some valuable time was wasted before they realized what a noble and patriotic soul I really am.

Gulliver had been originally shown to Serlin by an amazing little man named Joseph Burstyn, who immediately proceeded to demonstrate that it was possible to be simultaneously an aesthete and a tough negotiator. He not only persuaded the solemn Russians that, although they should, under no circumstances, have anything to do with a picture that wandered from the Party line, it would be perfectly all right for us to do so, particularly if they sold us the rights for American distribution for the incredibly low price of seven thousand dollars.

Burstyn and I proceeded to form a partnership for the distribution of *The New Gulliver* and other foreign films. My contribution was unbounded ignorance and limited capital; his, a wide acquaintance with the European market and something approaching genius in acquiring, editing and merchandising its product. When Joe discovers a picture he likes he becomes overwhelmingly and monogamously (temporarily) enamored of it to the exclusion of everything else in the world. During these sieges we would tiptoe around the stricken lover trying to carry on a hushed business having to do with matters out of his current world: trivia such as rival pictures which were competing with us, pictures which we were contemplating handling (or had been contemplating before Cupid conked him on the head), and pictures which Burstyn had once been in love with and which, with a little attention, were still capable of paying box-office returns. Personally, I was never capable of such single-minded devotion as to cool on a paying property.

In the preparation and exploitation of a picture, once Joe is enamored of it, he is so thorough and perfectionist in his methods that he reminds me of an actor I once heard of who, when he played Othello, used to black himself all over. Even in his days of wildest devotion, however, he rarely appears at his office before twelve noon, but once there he is apt to work all night. It could never be said of him, as Howard Dietz once said of himself when Nick Schenck complained that he came to work too late, "I can't deny it, but you must admit that I leave early."

Mayer-Burstyn struggled along importing excellent films like *Club de Femmes, Ballerina, Generals Without Buttons*, and many others, with mediocre results, until, in 1946, to the amazement of ourselves and everyone else in the industry, we hit the jackpot with an Italian feature, *Open City*. Its director, Roberto Rossellini, was, at the time I first saw the picture in Italy, practically unknown. In an article in the Italian magazine *Cinema* as late as 1948, he was referred to as "a director without special qualities who has not succeeded in making a name for himself." He produced *Open City* with practically no funds, with outdated negative and inadequate lighting and sound equipment. It cost only eighteen thousand dollars to make and Rossellini has always claimed that he lost money on it, although it should have earned him a fortune as it proved a terrific money-maker for distributors and exhibitors all over the world—except in Italy. It is quite possible, however, that he did lose on it, as Rossellini's business methods are, to put it mildly, somewhat confused.

His next picture, *Paisan*, for instance, created a genuine impasse as the American rights were sold both to us and to our leading competitor, Ilya Lopert. Eventually it was agreed that we should distribute it, with Lopert sharing in the profits. These were substantial, for *Paisan*, at least in America, surpassed *Open City*'s popularity and grossed for us close to a million dollars, breaking all previous records in this country for a foreign-language film.

A subsequent Rossellini production, *The Human Voice*, with Anna Magnani, has never been shown here and probably never will be, because of the half-dozen conflicting deals made by Rossellini or his agents for its distribution.

Rossellini works like Chaplin, without any prepared script or even a preliminary treatment. He uses only a brief summary of his projected sequences, which serves as a kind of road map. His method of selecting actors is similarly unorthodox. "I take them where I find them," he says, "working in factories or walking down the street." He also disdains sets as restrictive and static. On his first trip to Hollywood he looked at a huge construction of a battleship with a painted blue sky behind it, shook his head in vigorous disapproval and said, "There lies the corpse of movie making." He further felt that the big Hollywood studios were so concerned with camera angles, trick shots and elaborate lighting that as a result the basic vitality of stories and people was destroyed. After he returned to Rome he said of his visit, "Hollywood is a great place. I mean great like a sausage factory with lots of system that turns out fine sausages. In Italy I have no sausages but I have freedom."

These free-wheeling methods demanded a great deal of faith from anyone associated with Rossellini. Burstyn and I undertook to finance his production of a picture to be known as *Germany, Year Zero*. Every time we made an advance we wistfully asked what the picture was going to be about. We got almost the same answer as the small boy he had selected to play the leading role, who had the temerity to inquire, "What does the name *Germany, Year Zero* mean?" (We had wondered too.) "Until the picture is finished it is sufficient if I know what it means," was all the satisfaction little Mr. Inquisitive got.

After a suspenseful period, Burstyn and I finally gave up. The picture was eventually completed, actually financed in large measure by the more trustful French government.

Another Italian director, less temperamental than Rossellini, but equally passionate in his insistence on a direct and simple approach to life, is Vittorio de Sica, the man who made *Shoe-Shine*, *The Bicycle Thief* and *Miracle in Milan*. Like Rossellini, he prefers to pick his performers from nonprofessionals. "Fortunately," he says, "the good God has made people of every variety and if I search long enough I always find the one I'm looking for." During his quest for a character to play a dispirited role in a recent picture, de Sica saw just what he was after in an old man who was quietly strolling down the Via Veneto in Rome. He pounced on him and exclaimed, "I want you for an actor in my film." De Sica's find bristled and spiritedly announced that he was a retired brigadier general. "You have insulted me, sir," he added, brushing his sleeve where Vittorio had grabbed him. Fortunately, God had made another face suitable for the role. It was on the person of a college instructor who was amenable and de Sica was spared the embarrassment of having to resort to using an experienced actor.

On a recent trip to America, de Sica was asked what had become of the day laborer whom he had picked up and starred in *The Bicycle Thief*. In a tone that suggested a fate worse than death, he reported sadly that the man had become an actor. So, also, had the delightful amateur who played the part of his wife. "She now," said de Sica, "goes about with ostrich feathers down to her ankles."

In the twenties, de Sica was Italy's romantic idol of stage and screen. He was the local Rudolph Valentino and was regarded as such an irresistible lover that daughters of respectable families were warned against him, which helped to enhance his popularity. About those days of acclaim the great lover recently remarked, "When you are cast in that role night after night all you crave is old age. Physical decay is your only salvation." He is today far from decay. Well preserved and strikingly handsome, if the role were not so repugnant to him he could still give the romantic boys a run, and could probably put his countryman and contemporary, Ezio Pinza, out of the race altogether.

Much of the headache and some of the sport in handling foreign films are the battles with the various censorship agencies: municipal, state, federal, industry association and myriad pressure groups of every hue. The New York State Board of Censors refused a license to a delightful little

picture, *The Life of a Cat*, because it showed in close-up
the birth of a litter of kittens. One of the most charming
Mayer-Burstyn importations, *Generals Without Buttons*,
had some scenes in which little boys of five ran around
with their small derrières exposed. This was considered so
shocking that several boards insisted that the baby rears be
completely eliminated; others sanctioned a brief glimpse
provided it was not a close-up or even a medium shot.
That was how it had to be finally released. In the case of
Open City we were denied a Motion Picture Association
seal until eventually we yielded and eliminated a scene
showing a baby, obviously a boy, perched on a potty. *The
Bicycle Thief* again brought us into conflict with the Association, which insisted that another youngster—this time
one with an urge to relieve his bladder—be purged. This
Burstyn declined to do, and in spite of its universally
recognized merits *The Bicycle Thief* was never granted
the industry seal of approval.

The *Forgotten Village*, a tender, sensitive picture made
by Herbert Kline from the Steinbeck book about rural life
in Mexico, was barred by the New York Censors because
it contained scenes of childbirth. We appealed to the
Board of Regents, and my cousin, Morris Ernst, who has
devoted so much of his distinguished career to fighting for
civil liberties, spoke with such eloquence that the decision
was reversed and the picture was approved. Unfortunately,
after all the fighting and arguing, not to mention the expense, it did practically no business.

We won another Pyrrhic victory with a French film,
The Whirlpool, which told honestly but with delicacy the

story of a bridegroom, injured on his honeymoon in such a fashion as to render him impotent. The picture was eventually passed but so many cuts were made by censor boards that few could puzzle out, when the picture was publicly shown, why a man deeply in love with his newly acquired wife refused, after one apparently agreeable night, again to sleep by her side, or why his equally devoted newly acquired wife was so incredibly upset by an auto mishap as to start bestowing amorous glances on stalwart strangers. Some concluded she must be the afflicted one and that the accident had thrown her off her rocker.

My partnership with Burstyn lasted fifteen years, the longest period that any firm has survived the hazards of trying to cajole American audiences into patronizing foreign films. It is a matter of deep regret to me that although we purchased *The Miracle* while we were still partners, our association had come to an end when it was suppressed by the New York State Board of Regents, who for the first time in their history overruled a favorable judgment by the New York State Board of Censors. I had seen the picture played in Italy, where no one in that predominantly Catholic country had even intimated that it was of a sacrilegious nature. I believe that our basic freedom of expression is imperiled when religious, political or vigilante groups, however well-intentioned, pressure civil authorities into suppressing works of art or entertainment of which they disapprove. I feel as strongly about this when the film under attack is *Oliver Twist* as when it is *The Miracle*. Those whom a picture offends are free to talk against it, boycott it, even picket it, but they should not be permitted to prevent others from seeing it except in those rare cases where a "clear or present danger exists." Burstyn, with characteristic courage, carried *The Miracle* case to the Supreme Court, which, by unanimous decision, reversed the holdings of the New York State Board of Regents and the lower court. Nonetheless it implied that although words like "sacrilegious" cannot be freely bandied about, censorship statutes could still be drawn. As a consequence, state and local censor boards are still doing business at the old stand, although Burstyn's success has encouraged new legal attacks upon them. For the time being, however, the screen is still deprived of the freedom of expression prior to publication enjoyed by other media of communication.

When word first got around that I was dabbling in foreign "arty" pictures, my Broadway associates began to address me as Monsieur and Signor; Vincent Sardi of Sardi's Restaurant suddenly took to suggesting French wines for my lunch; an English tailor solicited my business and one columnist stated that the erstwhile Merchant of Menace was now a Merchant Prince. Mike Mok, then with the New York *Post*, reported that I was leading a double life selling gore on one corner and art on another.

In this dual role I have listened to much double-talk. There are many misconceptions about the foreign-film business. I have heard it repeatedly said that foreign films are far superior to Hollywood's; I have listened and agreed in part to Europe's advantages: shoe-string producers are fresher because they have to keep both ears to the ground. They have no extravagant salaries, no heavy overhead expenses and no long-term contracts with stars. Their industry is hitched not to the stars, as here, but to the directors. In the United States only two directors, Griffith and De Mille, have ever acquired reputations that carried any weight at the box office.

On the Continent the names of top directors are household words, picture making is subsidized with government grants and pictures can show at least a small profit with patronage running into the thousands rather than running into the millions. Not being geared up to mass production or mass appeal, nor traditionally wedded to the boy-meets-girl theme, European producers can afford to gamble with ideological and psychological problems, sex in its less saccharine manifestations, and new and experimental techniques. When not trying futilely to imitate Hollywood, they seek to catch and reflect the warmth and vitality of daily life with more candor and realism and less sentimentality and adolescent clichés than are customary in American films.

And yet as a man who has become cross-eyed from looking at innumerable European pictures, I must report that the number of excellent ones is pitifully small. The American intelligentsia, so quick to condemn Hollywood, so parrotlike in their assumption of the superiority of foreign films, are partially merely expressing their innate snobbishness and partially honestly, if naïvely, misled by the unremitting research of men like Burstyn, Lopert and Shapiro; modesty forbids my mentioning myself. Joe and I used to look at hundreds of French, Italian, Swedish and British films in an effort to cull out a few that were worthy of

importation. Semi-annually we ensconced ourselves un-
comfortably in a projection room in Montreal for a lengthy
session. Occasionally, we would have the Balboa-like thrill
of coming unexpectedly upon some superb cinematic masterpiece, but by and large, the pictures we looked at were
inferior to American product in story, acting and technical
proficiency. When I served in Germany at the end of
World War II in the strange capacity of passing upon
what pictures the German people could or could not see,
I had the same experience. I heartily recommend to those
who regard Hollywood as a petrified forest of decaying
formulae and escapist morasses, a closer acquaintance with
the product of Italy's Cinecitta, France's Joinville, or England's Denham.

Few of our imports were popular in their own "mature"
countries. Rossellini once said to me, "Our people have
had enough reality. Now they like to see Betty Grable." I
almost missed screening *The Bicycle Thief* when on a trip
to Italy, as theatregoers over there told me it was of little
interest. They cynically dismissed the plight of the hero
which so distressed American audiences. "What a boob!"
they said. "If somebody stole his bicycle he needn't have
lost his job. All he had to do was to rent another."

Burstyn and I even went so far as to avoid European
successes as a guide to the selection of product for American importation. We purchased *Ballerina*, which was so
complete a failure abroad that the producer would not even
bother to send us a print. We fooled him and screened it
in Montreal, but he was still under the agreeable impression
that he was taking advantage of our American ignorance

when we bought it for a ridiculously low sum. On the other hand, we died an ignominious death with the much-touted *Louise*, starring Grace Moore; *Lower Depths*, a well-acted rendition of Gorki's celebrated classic; and *Bataille du Rail*, the greatest of all French war documentaries.

As for the subtlety of foreign fare, *The Eternal Mask*, our second importation, came to us minus two reels. This unduly disturbed me but it did not upset the critics, who were greatly impressed by its at that time novel schizophrenic theme as well as its equally experimental photography. Indeed, some of them commented on the novel method in which it suggested, rather than told, all aspects of its story, and one reviewer particularly referred to the "foreign flair for significant omission."

We imported our next film, *Club de Femmes* (with Danielle Darrieux, then unknown in the United States), because of its youthful gaiety and charm and were a little surprised when it began to roll up excellent grosses. On investigation we discovered that it was being sold as a spicy Lesbian tale with intimations of indelicate relations between the adorable young women. Needless to say, it proved one of our profitable importations.

On the whole subject of Hollywood vs. Europe, in fact, I find myself becoming increasingly like a certain type of drinking man familiar to anyone who has ever stood for any length of time at a bar. He is the one who, after several brooding glances in your direction, finally moves alongside you and with a mournful sigh asks, "Are you married, friend?" If you say you are (or aren't, it makes little difference), he will buy you a drink and launch into a short address on the subject of put-upon man in a woman's world. If you murmur a "yes" or a "how true" or merely nod in sympathy at one or two of his points, you become an understanding and trusted friend and he is shortly telling you about his personal problems in this woman's world, namely his wife. He will list her shortcomings; usually she is extravagant, she is a know-it-all, she is spoiling the children, she has no organizational ability for running a house, and he is supporting all her relatives, all of whom are hoodlums.

If at about this stage in his list of criticisms you again nod in sympathy, you are apt suddenly to become his enemy. He can find fault with his own, he can call names, but if anyone else does—or if he even fancies it—he wants to fight. You have insulted the woman he loves, the mother of his children, the sacredness of his home, and the American flag. And he starts taking off his coat.

My attitude toward Hollywood is not too dissimilar. I can find fault with it but when a brash New Yorker or a spinsterly anthropologist, after a limited sojourn, start to display their wit and wisdom at its expense, I take off my coat in its defense.

It is the honest conviction of many worthy, though misinformed, people that a substantial segment of the public is being denied the privilege of seeing American pictures of a superior caliber because of the obstinacy and stupidity of the "often illiterate and usually corrupt" * movie moguls. I have had considerable contact over many years

* John Davenport, "Uneasy Dreams," *Observer*, Sept. 23, 1951.

with these gentlemen, and though along with the rest of us, Messrs. Skouras and Schenck, Zanuck and Zukor, et al., may have their shortcomings, the last thing in the world I would say about them is that they are illiterate, corrupt or inferior in business acumen to their intelligentsia assailants. The bulk of the pictures they make are rented on a basis of a percentage of exhibitor receipts and the fluctuations of those receipts afford a daily national barometer of what audiences accept and what they reject. If a large portion of the public really desires pictures with greater intellectual, social or artistic content, it can get them quickly by acting in the only fashion that any business enterprise, whether it makes pictures or pretzels, can understand. It can make them profitable.

In my thirty-odd years in the business, the American people have had plenty of opportunities to support such pictures and have, with disheartening frequency, failed to do so. Although I have helped to import many of the finest pictures that were brought into this country, I was able to maintain this activity only because I was simultaneously operating the Rialto Theatre, which consistently showed the worst. The profits on the bad pictures enabled me to stand the losses (or, to be more accurate, the lack of profits) on the good ones. Most of the highbrow critics of the industry are incorrigible optimists because they only write and speak about the demand for "mature" films. I am a mild pessimist because I have invested my money in them.

In the prewar days Warners distinguished themselves with a series of films dealing with the important issues of the day—*Juarez, Dr. Ehrlich's Magic Bullet, They Won't*

Forget and *Watch on the Rhine.* These fine productions
brought out reams of favorable critical comment but a
deplorable paucity of patrons. Warners were left with the
impression that they had done something disgraceful like
presenting American motherhood in a sordid light, and for
a long time thereafter they were understandably skittish
and sensitive about the whole subject of uplift.

As far back as 1934 I wrote a piece in *Liberty* entitled
"Why Hollywood Loses Money on Good Pictures," which
compared in painful detail the box-office receipts of such
intelligent productions as *Berkeley Square* and *Emperor
Jones* with the intake of such moronic efforts as *The Half-
Naked Truth* and *They Had to Get Married.* A short time
thereafter, I met Cecil B. DeMille, and he said, "Mr.
Mayer, how can you say good pictures lose money? My
pictures are invariably profitable." I have reported elsewhere that quick as a flash I responded, "But yours are the
run of DeMille pictures." (This, however, is a strictly truth-
ful book and I must admit that I did not think of it until
three hours later. Now having seen and succumbed to *The
Greatest Show on Earth* I am grateful for my delayed reaction.)

Walter Wanger once told me that in his memorable
career, receipts on his pictures had been in approximately
inverse ratio to their cinematic merits. The public responded to potboilers like *Arabian Nights* and *Canyon
Passage* but it was cold to masterpieces like *The Long
Voyage Home* and *Stagecoach.* Equally unprofitable were
such unforgettable pictures as William Wellman's *The Ox-
Bow Incident, Night Must Fall* with Robert Montgomery,

and John Huston's *The Treasure of Sierra Madre* with Humphrey Bogart.

Of course, there have been exceptions. How many depends upon a definition of what constitutes "maturity" in films, a study in semantics left in the limbo of uncertainty by their proponents. *The Lost Weekend, The Best Years of Our Lives, Henry V*, if they qualify, were all unquestioned box-office successes, although, I suspect, not entirely for reasons related to their intellectual content. Those who contend that there has been marked progress in recent time in the reception of more serious subjects are, I think, victims of wishful thinking.

Judging by the advertising and the results in the smaller, more conventional-minded communities, *Streetcar Named Desire*'s success in the larger cities was due more to a startling and uninhibited portrayal of sex degeneracy than to its artistic merits. *Death of a Salesman,* an equally mature subject but less closely involved with the intimacies of man and woman, has been a heartbreaking fiasco. If Paramount's prize-winning *A Place in the Sun* is to return its original investment it will have to do so out of its foreign revenue. Its domestic rentals will be insufficient.

Dore Schary, upon becoming head of the Metro studio, made a notable effort to raise that studio's adult batting average with a series of fine films, such as *Intruder in the Dust,* which so able a critic as Bosley Crowther of *The New York Times* called "one of the great cinematic dramas of our times." It proved one of the great cinematic flops of all times. Mr. Schary had to go back to the mines—profitable mines, I mean—such as *King Solomon's.*

Stanley Kramer, after leaving the U. S. Army, devoted himself to making, with great skill and unusual economy, the type of pictures for which the intelligentsia pleads. In 1951 he fashioned, with rare courage and competency, *The Men*, a film about paraplegic veterans. Archer Winsten of the New York *Post* termed it "superb, popular entertainment." Certainly it was superb. Certainly it was not popular.

In 1949 Universal was over four million dollars in the red. By 1951 its red corpuscles had been reactivated with a profit of over five million before taxes. This was largely due to the *Ma and Pa Kettles*, a series about which I cannot write knowingly as I have never been able to sit through one of them. They cost about five hundred thousand dollars each to make and, although they play almost exclusively in small towns and neighborhood theatres, gross as high as two million, three hundred thousand dollars. Comparing the profits accruing from them to Universal's results when it dallied with the world of fantasy in *Harvey*, you can judge for yourself in what direction its executives are apt to angle their future production schedules.

Similarly, Paramount redeemed the heavy loss it suffered with William Wyler's exquisite *The Heiress* when it released De Mille's *Samson and Delilah*, which will gross approximately eleven million dollars. The average film plays to an audience of about thirteen million people but *Samson and Delilah* should triple that figure. It would appear as if what the industry thrives on is more Victor Matures rather than more mature pictures.

Another incredible bonanza of 1951 was *At War With*

the Army. In the face of a withering barrage from the reviewers, *The Army* wrecked the nonholiday box-office record for the New York Paramount Theatre with an opening week of $110,000 and then proceeded to wreak similar havoc across the entire countryside. Sometimes, as I dejectedly observe the good receipts for what good people call bad pictures and the bad receipts for what they call good, I am reminded of Henry Mencken's dour dictum: "No one ever went broke underestimating the taste of the American public."

An indomitable optimist, however, like the distinguished critic Gilbert Seldes, is not so easily discouraged. He contends the fault is not so much with the taste of the public as with the distribution practices of the major companies. "They ought," he says, "to play the adult pictures in the little theatres, and I imagine the adultery ones in the big theatres." Prejudiced as I am by a financial stake in several small houses, I heartily agree that pictures are frequently booked into inappropriate theatres. The problem, however, of inadequate public support lies far deeper than any distribution practices. Mayer-Burstyn showed *The Quiet One* in the most select small theatres of America. The movie critics rallied to its support with the unanimously enthusiastic reviews which this gem of a picture so fully deserved. Our final national gross was less than that of many Hollywood shorts!

In 1950 *The Titan* was voted the best foreign film of the year by the National Board of Review but in spite of this endorsement and that of the press, this epoch-making picture about the life and works of Michelangelo has just recovered the modest cost of less than twenty thousand dollars involved in its American re-editing.

The same fate is overtaking three outstandingly mature films which I am now distributing in the art theatres in conjunction with Edward Kingsley: *The Magic Garden,* a South African tale enlivened by the haunting musical score of "The Pennywhistle Blues"; *Jour de Fête,* a French comedy reminiscent of Chaplin's earliest and best days; and *The Young and the Damned,* of which Alton Cook of the *World-Telegram and Sun* wrote: "A film of terrifying power and brutality. . . . It seems to be life itself directing." The countries of their origin and the nature of the merits of these three pictures vary, but not their disappointing reception at the American box offices.

The only sensational successes scored by Burstyn and myself in the fifteen years in which we were engaged in business were with pictures whose artistic and ideological merits were aided and abetted at the box office by their frank sex content. These we were able to exhibit profitably in big theatres as well as small. *Open City* was generally advertised with a misquotation from *Life* adjusted so as to read: "Sexier than Hollywood ever dared to be," together with a still of two young ladies deeply engrossed in a rapt embrace, and another of a man being flogged, designed to tap the sadist trade. The most publicized scene in *Paisan* showed a young lady disrobing herself with an attentive male visitor reclining by her side on what was obviously not a nuptial couch. *The Bicycle Thief* was completely devoid of any erotic embellishments, but the exhibitors sought to atone for this deficiency with a highly imaginative sketch of a young lady riding a bicycle. This was not good, or bad, enough, and in spite of the critics' rave reviews it did far less business than either of the others.

In 1951 I helped to import *Seven Days to Noon*, an English film dealing with the plight of a high-minded scientist who has planned to devote his life to benefiting humanity but finds that his research work is apparently dedicated to its destruction. Half-crazed, he threatens to blow up London and is apprehended only at the last moment after the whole city has been evacuated, when he pauses to kneel in prayer in a deserted church. It was a thriller, it was moving, it received heart-warming critical praise all over the country and the 1951 Oscar as the best story of the year. With the exception of New York City it died. While it was dying, films of a highly sexy nature like *Manon* and *Latuko* were, in territories unencumbered by censors, holding them out in long queues at the so-called art theatres. Simultaneously, *Bitter Rice* was breaking even *Open City* and *Paisan* records. It had no cinematic merit but it had a bountifully proportioned leading lady, Silvana Mangano, and, as Howard Hughes said of Jane Russell in *The Outlaw*, there were two good reasons why every man wanted to see it.

Much has been made by hostile critics of the fact that approximately two-thirds of movie attendance comes from people under thirty-five years of age. I cannot see, however, why this should be a source of surprise to anybody. If I go to a football game, or into a store that sells sheet music or to a night club (I never do, but if I did), I am surrounded almost exclusively by young people. If we can generalize about such matters, youth likes to go out; middle age likes to stay home. Youth is eager for entertainment; middle age prefers its slippers and a pipe by the fireside. I do not agree, however, for one moment that on youth's shoulders alone rests the responsibility for the popularity of some tawdry, trashy pictures any more than that it is responsible for the popularity of some tawdry, trashy books and plays.

Actually, I have more faith in the taste of people under thirty than of those over forty-five. As we grow older most of us get into a mental rut in which we are apt to accept the entertainment formulae of our youth as the correct ones and arbitrarily to reject the new and the experimental. It was young audiences rather than old who first welcomed Disney and Chaplin, just as in music they were the first to hail Wagner, or in poetry, Walt Whitman, or in painting, Cézanne.

The vast New York high school auditorium where the organization known as Cinema 16 holds its showings of strange avant-garde documentaries is composed ninety-five per cent of people not only under thirty-five but under twenty-five. To my hardening arteries many of the unusual pictures they show border on the ludicrous, but that is exactly how my dear mother felt thirty years ago about *Caligari*.

Actually, Hollywood cannot fairly be accused of catering exclusively to any single age or interest group. It is outgrowing the theory that it can appeal only to the lowest common denominator to make a profitable return upon its investment. It seeks, maybe not always successfully, but to the best of its ability, to speak to every segment of the American people. Included in its 1951-52 releases were:

The African Queen
Alice in Wonderland
An American in Paris
Angels in the Outfield
The Big Sky
The Brave Bulls
Bright Victory
Captain Horatio Hornblower
David and Bathsheba
Death of a Salesman
Decision Before Dawn
Detective Story
Five Fingers
Fourteen Hours
The Great Caruso
The Greatest Show on Earth
High Noon
I Was a Communist
Ivanhoe
Limelight
People Will Talk
A Place in the Sun
Quo Vadis
The Red Badge of Courage
Showboat
The Story of Robin Hood

A *Streetcar Named Desire*
Viva *Zapata*

I do not suggest that these are pictures which future ages will cherish, nor do I expect anyone, myself included, to be enthusiastic over every one of them. What I do maintain, however, is that in the face of censorship restrictions, pressure groups, police authorities and, recently, even license commissioners, they represent a wider general appeal and a higher average merit than that supplied by popular fiction magazines, by the radio, or by television, and fully as high as that of current books or drama.

The results with these films and with all the others released last year, from the incredibly successful *The Greatest Show on Earth* to the equally incredible debacle of *The Red Badge of Courage*, were carefully appraised in the offices of every major picture producer. Their studies are not confined to Hollywood pictures. English and foreign films are given the same meticulous scrutiny. When we imported *Open City*, Rossellini was catapulted overnight into world-wide demand. Metro-Goldwyn-Mayer cabled an offer to the Boulting Brothers, producers and directors of *Seven Days to Noon*, almost simultaneously with its successful New York première. In the field of distribution and exhibition there may have been collusion and conspiracy among the picture companies, but in their production the fiercest competition exists for talent and for successful means of employing it.

You may deprecate the box office as a standard of merit but in the words of an insignificant writer with whom I find myself constantly in amazing agreement: "It is an unfailing barometer of what we want in our heart of hearts —frippery or meaning, shadow or substance. The responsibility [if I may continue to quote from myself in *Theatre Arts*] for making the motion picture a mighty instrument of mankind's hope and salvation lies not with producers, distributors or exhibitors, not even with authors or directors, but with the audience. If we support, not with chatter but with cash, not in the drawing room but in the theatre auditorium, those films which give a true account of our honest problems and highest aspirations, we can make our motion pictures a symbol and token of all striving humanity —a living voice speaking among the people."

Or, in less lofty language, I think a lot of pictures are good and a lot more of them will be good as soon as the public wants them. I also think a lot of movie people are bright in the head, and with a little more encouragement would be glad to demonstrate it more frequently. I have written of the good old days but I am not at all nostalgic about them. I think the present days, movie-wise if not otherwise, are reasonably good, and I am unreasonable enough to believe that the future will be even better.

· XIII ·

CURRENT CONDITIONS in the movie industry provide little apparent support for my optimism. When I returned from Europe in the late fall of 1949, I was greeted at the airport by several of my motion picture friends, their conversation, if not their Cadillacs, draped in sackcloth and ashes. During my absence, in the words of *Variety*, our business had declined from "sensational" to "merely colossal." My partners in a small suburban theatre, which over the years had rarely shown a profit of less than forty thousand dollars annually, reported we would be fortunate to break even. One member of the delegation had a sister with six children. "The kids," he told me, "don't even use their passes any more." Unless patronage picked up, a large number of the theatres, or so I was told, would have to be converted into garages or into homes for indigent movie men. Actu-

Business had declined from "sensational" to "merely colossal."

ally the number of theatres continued to increase until 1951 when, with a total of over twenty-three thousand, the National Production Authority ordered the discontinuance of further theatre construction.

In the meantime, however, box-office receipts continued to nosedive from "merely colossal" to only "excellent." By 1951, in spite of an increase of twenty-three per cent in our national population and the highest rate of employment in our history, theatre receipts had declined from a high of one billion, five hundred and twelve million to a low of approximately one billion, two hundred million. The pre-tax earnings of the major producing companies, which in 1946 amounted to two hundred and four million, had sagged to one hundred. Vanished were the boom days when all that a manager had to do, or so we gaily wisecracked, was to open the doors and quickly step out of the way to keep from being run over by the stampede of eager customers. Our share of all of the money spent for amusement in America had dwindled from an astronomic eighty-five per cent to less than seventy-three per cent and was still on the toboggan. Weekly attendance, once considerably overestimated (in accordance with the best movie traditions) at ninety million, had fallen to a reported fifty-five (probably also an exaggeration), still a big slice of America, but not enough to maintain the industry in the lavish fashion to which it had become accustomed.

To this dismal picture, however, there are three exceptions, all of them worth noting, as showing that where movie houses meet a public need they have nothing to fear except fear itself. A few fortunate long-run theatres like the Music Hall, playing the pick of Hollywood product, are doing better business than ever before in their history. Art houses, such as the Sutton, for instance, specializing in choice English and foreign pictures, are increasing in number and prosperity. Most sensational of all, a new phenomenon, the drive-in, is multiplying and flourishing. Originally these outdoor theatres were disparagingly referred to by conservative competitors as "passion pits with pix," but actually they represent the acme of respectable conduct and owe their popularity to their suitability for the family trade: the kiddies, who, minus the services of a sitter, can sleep in comfort in the rear seat of the car; Dad, who loathes parking and dressing up; and Grandpa and Grandma, who shun queues and dark aisles. According to *Variety*, there are even canoe-ins, bike-ins and fly-ins.

What are the reasons for the catastrophic decrease in the business of all other types of theatres? Most movie men will, I think, be inclined to agree that the rise of television—both the money spent for sets as well as the time devoted to them—has been the primary cause, and substantiating statistics from varying sections of the country indicate convincingly close relation between television infiltration and box-office decline. A contributing factor has been the rise in the popularity of competitive entertainments, night baseball in particular. Simultaneously, the success of the government lawsuits against the producing, distributing, theatre-owning companies has created problems in the marketing of films with which the industry was ill prepared to grapple. Another handicap has been the failure to build up attractive new screen personalities to replace the waning popularity of the famous stars of yesterday. These and other factors have united to create conditions of grim anxiety throughout the industry. And yet, although it may be small satisfaction to those whose survival is threatened, I am confident that in the long run these conditions will prove a blessing in disguise and help, rather than hinder, the welfare of the industry. The dark clouds that now obscure the silver screen have, when closely examined, a silver lining.

To this comforting conviction there is one grave exception. No creative art can function in an atmosphere of fear. Great pictures cannot be made by conformers—and if there is any doubt of this, the fate of the once-thriving film industries of Germany and Russia is proof. Although the plotting and intrigues of the Communists in Hollywood accomplished close to zero, there is no room for their duplicity and treachery in a medium of public opinion. But on the other hand, before the infamy of Communism became apparent there was no crime in hoping that it might offer relief to the needy and the oppressed. Some generous and high-minded souls were misled into joining the Party and even more became members of organizations now justly regarded as subversive. The men and women, however, who in their youth question established economic and political institutions are apt also to examine and re-examine orthodox picture-making procedures—stories, directors, acting, technique. Any creative industry that permits pressure groups—however well-intentioned—to drive such minds from its ranks is imperiling its future health and usefulness.

On the other hand, I am not at all disturbed by the waning box-office appeal of the great stars of yesterday. Gary Cooper, Clark Gable, Bob Hope, Jimmie Stewart, Humphrey Bogart—gallantry prevents mention of their female contemporaries—are no longer glamorous lads but middle-aged citizens beginning to bulge or bald, better cast as fond fathers than as passionate lovers.

Recently a teen-age boy remarked to me, "We fellows are tired of seeing girls of our age being made love to by men of your age." Ezio Pinza gave a heartening (to all men over fifty) demonstration on Broadway of sustained sex appeal, but on Main Street he was dismissed as a portly gentleman trying to act younger than was seemly.

Fortunately, however, the patron's first question today is no longer who is in the picture but what is in it. The public flocked to see *The Great Caruso* not because of Mario Lanza but because people loved the music. Kirk Douglas did not make *The Champion*; a writer named Ring Lardner did. Columbia is said to have considered Rita Hayworth for the lead in *Born Yesterday* in order to assure it the success which her name would provide. An actress known to Broadway but unheard of in the hinterlands, Judy Holliday, played the part and won the year's Oscar for the best acting job. It was not planned that way, and still is bitterly lamented by producers and exhibitors alike who have always regarded the presence of big names in pictures as in the nature of an insurance policy. In the long run, however, their escape from the horse-and-buggy system of hitching their vehicles to a star will prove a godsend both to them and to all lovers of good pictures.

Authors, directors, technicians will come into their own as we bid farewell forever to the starry shadows that Broncho Billy, John Bunny and Mary Pickford cast upon the screen.

The fading of the stars was deplored by the movie magnates, but they fought the government antitrust suit with the ardor of crusaders. The Department of Justice first filed its suit in equity against the eight major companies in 1938, but it took thirteen years of litigation before the five major companies bowed to the inevitable and entered into consent decrees with the government entailing the complete separation of their affiliated theatres from their production and distribution activities. Paramount even went so far in its acceptance of the new order that the private elevator in the Paramount Building connecting sales and theatre offices was discontinued.

In addition, many trade practices long regarded as essential to the mysterious rights and rites of film distribution were found by the court to be destructive of free competition. Among these are circuit booking of films, through which powerful buyers obtained preference over independent exhibitors regardless of the size, location or condition of their theatres; the fixing of admission prices by distributors; "blind buying" (the rental of films without their first being made available for screening by all exhibitors); and excessive clearances by which a substantial period of time elapses between the first and the subsequent showing of pictures.

Most drastic of all, the court abolished block booking on the ground that it forced inferior pictures on exhibitors, and compelled them to devote so much of their playing time to the product of the major distributors that they had no available dates for films produced by independents, regardless of their merit.

The effect of block booking has always been controversial. Blockheaded reformers suffer from the impression that exhibitors are straining at the leash to play the sort of pictures uplifters rather than patrons like, and are only restrained by the wicked machinations of the evil distributors. Actually, this is far from the case. A good many years ago, when the major companies, in a short-lived outburst of generosity, lightened the burden of block booking to permit a limited number of cancellations, a fine film like Barrie's *Quality Street* received 4837 cancellations and *The Great Garrick* had 3389 as compared to 15 for *The Last Gangster* and 220 for *Her Jungle Love*.

The reformers also suffer from an obsession that all B pictures are bad. Actually, a B picture is only the trade term for an inexpensive film, and cheap pictures and poor ones have in the past been no more invariably synonymous than expensive pictures and good. It is not always necessary to spend a fortune to make splendid features, as Leo McCarey's *Make Way for Tomorrow*, Garson Kanin's *A Man to Remember*, Val Lewton's *Curse of the Cat People*, Elia Kazan's *Boomerang* and a host of others amply demonstrate.

All considered, however, it cannot be denied that block booking stimulated the production of an incredible amount of unmitigated trash. B pictures were assigned to the supervision of men who conceived their function to be that of copycats of past successes. In no other industry in the world has so high an average of the product been deliberately conceived and manufactured with such cynical disregard of its value to the retailer or its appeal to the ultimate consumer. Some companies admittedly pursued a policy of producing a half-dozen cheaters for every quality film on their schedule. All considered, in the light of the experience of the past twenty years, it can safely be deduced that as far as the motion picture industry is concerned (and I would not be surprised, as far as all industries are concerned), practices destructive of a free market are not conducive to the welfare of the community or to that of the industry involved. For four years neither Paramount nor M-G-M produced a single picture that lost money, although they turned out many that were admittedly of little value. Security through artificial devices is as debilitating to an economy as reliance on a Maginot Line is to a nation.

The consent decrees entered into between the government and the film companies mean the opening of the picture industry to a far keener battle for playing time on the screens of the nation than it has known since its pie-throwing pioneer days. To old-fashioned souls who pin their hopes for progress on the forces inherent in competition rather than in cartels, closed markets or other restrictive trade practices, this appears a step in the right direction.

As usual, however, where sound economic laws have been flouted, the pains of readjustment are severe and prolonged. The innocent suffer along with the guilty. Exhibitors who have been trained to rely on a large volume of films for an uncritical audience must painfully acquire new policies, new methods of merchandising, new patrons and even maybe new uses for a large number of marginal theatres. The theatres that remain, or those that will be newly constructed (now that the NPA is raising its building restrictions), will, for their own preservation, have to experiment with the use of large-screen television, third-dimension, convex screens designed to prevent distortion, improved acoustics and sight lines, maybe with reserved seats, and surely, I hope, with single features. The show houses of the future will require adjustable chairs (the new Beekman actually has rocking chairs!), more leg room and ample space to permit the serving, under agreeable conditions, of light refreshments, most of them being already knee-deep in candy, popcorn, ice cream and soft drinks. They will offer better parking facilities and higher standards of comfort and service. Only in this fashion will they persuade deserters to television that be it ever so humble there is no place like a theatre.

And the number of these deserters is legion. In five years the dark cloud of television has been transformed from a faint disturbance on the distant ether to a raging storm over most of America. Almost overnight on the rooftops of our residential sections, particularly those of the lower-income or middle-income groups, angular, Calder-like antennae have blossomed forth, suggestive of some menacing new totalitarian insignia. By 1949 television accounted for fifteen per cent of the total broadcast audience. Moving with startling rapidity, one year later it was forty-nine and six-tenths per cent. A competent if not entirely neutral observer, David Sarnoff, predicts that by 1955 there will be twenty-five hundred channels and fifty million sets in the homes of America. What was formerly a man's castle is fast becoming his movie theatre.

Anyone who suffers from the delusion that such an invasion is not materially altering the theatre attendance habits of the American public should, as Sam Goldwyn is supposed to have said of a friend who was being psychoanalyzed, have his head examined. Television is free, or at least once a set has been purchased, it appears to be free; it can be seen without using a bus, your car or your legs. Its capacity to cover sporting events such as prizefights, baseball and political conventions makes it every man's delight. To the kiddies it brings more horror and bloodshed than their mamas ever let them see in the theatre.

A Washington, D. C., survey gravely announced a decline of seventy-two per cent in movie patronage by owners of television sets. If such a so-called research job were factual, the motion picture business could only have been a multibillion-dollar industry, but it was reprinted in such reliable journals as *The New York Times* and the *Wall Street Journal*. More scientific studies seemed to establish that every three per cent of TV saturation results in a box-office decline of one per cent, with a considerable leveling off after a saturation of sixty per cent is attained.

What will happen now that the freeze on new stations has been lifted and 2053 more are scheduled to sprout all over the country? What will happen with the inevitable advent of color television, larger screens, more skillful and diversified programs, improved reception and a greater reservoir of creative talent? No one requires a crystal ball with sound attachment to see and hear the explosion in the household of 1955 when the suggestion is offered that Father undergo the vicissitudes of parking and maybe standing in line to pay admission for the family to see the average B movie, instead of remaining comfortably, cost-lessly, and coatlessly in his favorite easy chair, watching and hearing old films and new controversies as long as the spirit moves, and then turning a dial to catch something else or maybe just to catch a few welcome winks of sleep. Romantically inclined young people can pet in the parlor, hugging the console and each other far more comfortably and less conspicuously than in any theatre mezzanine.

Some hostile observers have gone so far as to predict, with every evidence of satisfaction, that seventy-five per cent of the movie theatres will have to close, but these cheerful prophets of doom can be substantially discounted. As long as television remains harnessed to advertising budg-ets it cannot hope to compete with Hollywood in produc-tion values or as a purchaser of outstanding plays and novels. Even under the existing unpropitious conditions, smash hits like Paramount's *The Greatest Show on Earth*, or Metro's *Quo Vadis*, look headed for grosses of at least twelve million dollars. With such potential returns, movie producers can gamble millions without wincing. Their tele-vision rivals are not quite in that class yet. They wince. But even if they had the wherewithal, television, handi-capped by a comparatively small screen, could never reproduce the vast spectacle pictures which, next to crime and sex, have been the movies' strongest asset.

Visualize, for example, some of the sensational tourney scenes in *Ivanhoe*, or the ballet from *An American in Paris*, on a twenty-inch home screen rather than on a twenty-foot theatre screen. My daughter said to me one day that she did not care very much for television. When I asked her why, she replied, "I can't get much excited about any man who is only the size of my foot."

In addition to all of these limitations, television must, by its nature, be serviced by writers and directors capable of turning out hundreds of shows per week. When Edwin Porter went to work for Zukor in 1912 and Zukor told him he wanted six pictures a year, Porter said, "There isn't that much talent in the world." To meet television's future demands, I am equally certain there isn't that much talent in the universe.

Even if there were, there would still be trouble as television viewers quickly tire of its personalities. Nobody wants to see the same visitors in his drawing room too frequently. New performers appear, enjoy a quick popularity and, instead of lasting for years as in the movies, are frequently through in a brief period. Aware of this, most of the talented entertainers (the majority of whom are recruits from the older forms of show business) are now spacing their appearances judiciously, leaving a lot of available time open to be filled with entertainers of such minor talent, if any, that many customers in self-defense are driven back into movie houses.

Under its present setup, television has inherited from

radio that medium's chronic headache: Will the program sell the sponsor's goods? In their most trying moments, the movies, at least, were never hog-tied with the double duty of having to please both an audience seeking a good time and a manufacturer seeking additional customers.

A number of suggestions have been offered as to how television can escape its present thralldom to the budgets of its sponsors. All of these are predicated on some toll-vision system by which a stay-at-homer can automatically decode a scrambled picture signal on his screen and in this fashion see some movie he is willing to pay for. The most publicized of these devices is Phonevision, which, as experimented with in Chicago, had a tie-up with the telephone company and charged one dollar at the end of the month for every picture it unscrambled.

Paramount has acquired control of Telemeter, which clears the screen through the deposit of the required quarters or half-dollars in a coin slot, and Skiatron has a somewhat similar scheme. The proponents of all these devices argue that in one night, by bringing the box office into the living room, a picture could gross more millions than it would in a month of theatre showings. They all, however, present economic, technical and governmental problems which make their early application highly improbable. They run, moreover, as all forms of television do, counter to the human need for gregariousness—we and the monkeys are the most gregarious animals on earth—to the contagious enjoyment that comes from laughing together, crying together, shuddering together, hating the villain together. They fail to satisfy the feminine desire to step out in new clothes and among new people after a day at home devoted to the kiddies and the kitchen. As an added hazard, they challenge American mechanical ingenuity in discovering methods of unscrambling without shelling out.

It is possible that pay-as-you-see television may someday replace second runs or serve as an ideal method for big companies to cash in on reissues of their old pictures. I do not think, however, that exhibitors, local merchants or transportation companies need spend any sleepless nights contemplating what will happen when the glowing lights of the theatre marquee on Main Street fade away forever.

After all the excitement subsides, television will be accepted by movie makers and exhibitors as radio was, and transformed from an antagonist into an ally. Once again I believe that the thesis of this book—if it has anything so pretentious as a thesis—is about to be demonstrated in action and that movies will move forward neither through careful advance planning nor through flashes of brilliant improvisation, but as a consequence of developments which we fought and regarded as close to catastrophic. If, as Oscar Wilde says, "Each man kills the thing he loves," it is equally plausible that the things he hates are his salvation. Television has already served to develop popular new performers like Martin and Lewis for the screen. It will prove the ideal medium for advertising coming attractions. Its compulsory experiments in economical production short cuts will have a chastening influence on studio extravagance. It will eventually hugely expand the appeal of motion picture theatres by enabling them to show in actual color, as already demonstrated by Spyros Skouras' Eidophor equipment, not only prizefights, baseball games and crime investigations, but the opera, symphony orchestras, the UN or Congress in session, maybe great historical events like a new President delivering his inaugural address. Musical hits like *The King and I*, or great performances like Olivier and Leigh in *Caesar and Cleopatra* and *Anthony and Cleopatra*—Two on the Nile, we called it—will be shown while they are still on Broadway. It is highly possible that special productions will be created to be televised under more propitious conditions than any legitimate theatre stage permits for simultaneous screenings in thousands of theatres all over the country. It is my honest conviction that the cinema, far from being on the brink of disaster, is actually on the threshold of developments that can assure its supremacy as the greatest entertainment and educational institution that the world has ever known.

With applied intelligence, television can prove to be the spark which revitalizes the entire conception of modern theatre operation, and there will be sore need for such revitalization. Under the new system of "bidding" for pictures which the distributors claim the court decree entails, rentals demanded for preferred product will probably mount to such altitudes that lachrymose exhibitors will refer back nostalgically to the good old days of '52. In the face of increased competition for the entertainment dollar, however, the burden of these and other increased costs cannot be passed on to the public in the form of higher admission prices. Indeed, it is probable that they will decline.

To survive, theatre operators will have to shine up the resourceful and indefatigable showmanship on which the early success of "fillums" was founded. The producers also will be confronted with arduous readjustments. Not all of them will emerge from the ordeal of fire and firing. Those who do so, however, may, partially as a consequence of their defeat by the Department of Justice, regain many times over the money they spent to avoid it. Just as we have seen the runs of smash hits in New York stretch out for many months and even to years, we will find the playing time of successful pictures all over the country extending far beyond anything now deemed remotely conceivable. Fewer pictures will be made, but they will have to be more popular than ever before.

Not long ago a friend sent me a copy of a magazine article which read in part as follows:

"The motion picture business today is in a bad way. Neither the producers nor the theatres are making money and the critics are justly condemning most of the current films. The fault lies partially with the exhibitor but the primary responsibility rests upon the producer because he is not producing good enough pictures. Unless he does so, and does so promptly, the movie business cannot hope long to endure."

That article appeared in *Photoplay Magazine* for October, 1918.

I have been reading similar lugubrious pieces ever since I entered the business and fully expect to continue to do so for the balance of my days. They don't worry me one bit.

CAST OF CHARACTERS

256

G

Gable, Clark, 244
Garbo, Greta, 6
Garden, Mary, 8, 11, 12
Gaynor, Janet, 149
Glyn, Elinor, 71
Godsol, F. J., 39-44, 46-48, 50, 51, 54-59
Golden, Edward, 196, 197
Goldenson, Leonard, 164
Goldwyn, Sam, 8-15, 24-27, 35-42, 44, 47, 83, 170, 249
Gomez, Juan Vincente, President, 174
Gordon, Nathan, 81, 96
Gorki, Maxim, 226
Grable, Betty, 225
Graham, Lillie, 182
Grainger, Edmund, 49
Grainger, James, 42
Grant, Cary, 120
Gray, William, 81
Green, Abel, 89
Greene, Graham, 134
Griffith, D. W., 150, 156, 157, 224

H

Hackett, James K., 147
Hale, Chief, 142, 144
Hammerstein, Arthur, 184
Hammerstein Oscar I, 180, 181
Hammerstein, Oscar II, 180, 181
Hammerstein, William, 181-184
Hampton, Benjamin, 155
Harlow, Jean, 149
Harris, John H., 22
Harris, John P., 22-24
Hart, Bill, 156
Havilland, Olivia de, 210, 211

Hayes, Helen, 128, 149
Hays, Will, 9, 119, 123, 176, 192
Hayworth, Rita, 221, 244
Hearst, William Randolph, 185, 186
Hecht, Ben, 203
Heifitz, Jascha, 170
Hertz, John, 67
Hoblitzelle, Carl, 164
Hollander, William, 72
Holliday, Judy, 244
Hope, Bob, 244
Hopkins, Miriam, 123, 128, 192
Houdini, 132
Howard, Leslie, 149
Hughes, Howard, 134, 234
Hughes, Rupert, 11
Hulsey, E. H., 158, 159
Huston, John, 230

I

Ince, Thomas H., 155

J

Jacobs, Joe, 9
Jannings, Emil, 125, 126
Jones, Jennifer, 210

K

Kahn, Otto, 162
Kalem Company, 50, 51
Kanin, Garson, 246
Karloff, Boris, 130
Katz, Sam, 63-65, 68, 72-74, 93-96, 99, 102, 106, 107, 109-111, 114, 145, 163, 164
Katzman, Sam, 194
Kaufman, Les, 72

ABOUT THE AUTHOR

*Arthur Mayer was born in the metropolis of Demopolis, Ala-
bama, more years ago than he is prepared to admit. Although
he attended Harvard College, he claims to have acquired what
little education he has in the motion picture industry. The
best teachers he has ever known were Sam Goldwyn, Adolph
Zukor of Paramount and the patrons of his theatres.*

*He has handled the advertising campaigns which helped to
establish such famous stars as Mae West and Marlene Dietrich.
He has operated theatres in all parts of the United States, including the Rialto on Broadway, where he instituted the profitable policy of playing nothing but bad pictures. To salve his
conscience he has been active in the importation of many of
the most famous foreign films, such as* Open City, Paisan, The
Bicycle Thief *and* Seven Days to Noon.

*During the war years he helped organize and operate the
War Activities Committee of the Motion Picture Industry,
which gave thousands of films free of charge to the military
forces; served as Film Consultant to the Secretary of War and
as personal representative of the Chairman of the American
Red Cross. For these services he was awarded the Medal for
Merit, the highest civilian award.*

*After the war he was appointed Chief of the Motion Picture
Branch of Military Government in Germany, which position
he resigned in 1949.*

Upon his return to the United States he was elected Exec-

utive Vice President of the Council of Motion Picture Organ-
izations, in which capacity he helped to organize and conduct
the recent "Movietime, U.S.A." campaign. He declines, how-
ever, to accept credit for the slogan "Movies Are Better Than
Ever."

In his moments of leisure he has been associated with such
memorable documentary films as Crisis, The City, *and* The
Forgotten Village; *has conducted an educational film project*
for the Motion Picture Association of America; acted as ad-
viser to a group of textbook publishers for their "Teaching
Films Survey," and has served as film consultant for every con-
ceivable organization interested in the use of the movies, from
the E.C.A. to the Planned Parenthood Association.

He has written of his experiences in theatres of war and
theatres of peace in such magazines as Harper's, Liberty, The
Saturday Review of Literature, Esquire, Theatre Arts, *and* The
New Republic.

Until he started to write a book about his movie experiences,
he had a devoted wife, children who respected his judgment,
and a host of friends.